JEFFERSON
AND RELIGION

JEFFERSON AND RELIGION

Eugene R. Sheridan

Preface by Martin E. Marty

THOMAS JEFFERSON MEMORIAL FOUNDATION

Monticello Monograph Series

1998

The Thomas Jefferson Memorial Foundation, Inc.

This publication was made possible by a gift from Mr. and Mrs. Martin S. Davis.

Portrait of Thomas Jefferson
by Thomas Sully
(Thomas Jefferson Memorial Foundation, Inc.)

PREFACE

*F*EW CITIZENS today think of their presidents as theologians. Yet if theology means interpreting the life of a people in the light of a transcendent reference, then certain public figures serve well. The two American presidential classic theologians are Thomas Jefferson and Abraham Lincoln.

Much of Jefferson's interest in religion was of a generic, broadly philosophical sort. He could be described as a Deist, which is to say, he believed in natural law, in natural reason, in a God accessible without the medium of an inspired scripture. He could be quite contentious about traditional, dogmatic, or sectarian religions, and, in the mood of many Enlightenment figures, was critical of "priestcraft" and institutional religion.

Jefferson could not complete his theological or moral program, however, without relating to the religion of the vast majority of American citizens. That meant the religion of the Bible, and for the near-monopoly of Christians, it meant the New Testament, the gospels, and their central figure Jesus, whom he greatly admired. So he dealt with the gospels, as Eugene R. Sheridan so well demonstrates in this essay, by editing their contents and giving them his own distinctive order.

The gospels are four short collections about rabbi Jesus of Nazareth, who to Christians is Jesus Christ, the exalted Lord. They impart all, every word, that the Christian church believes we know about Jesus. (There are some gospels that did not quite make it into the Bible, and they may offer some glimpses. But the believing community never had enough confidence in such collections to put them forward as belonging to the biblical canon.) Non-believing contemporaries of Jesus, "outsiders," paid no attention to his life. And the gospels that we have, compiled by "insiders," collect memories and documents a generation or more after he lived among the disciples. With little wonder, such documents are precious to believers. They like them intact.

Few leave them intact, however. Ministers preach on short passages, parables or sayings. Composers write oratorios on them. Artists draw images from the gospels. Scholars chop them finely, straining to determine what is truly historical in them, how they got put together, what is their literary character, and in what way they might be thought of as the word of God. Believers have always been excerpting them and extracting from them. But they tend to be suspicious of anyone else who does the extracting.

The same readers who might stand in awe of a president who was so curious and so serious as to put together collections of extracts called *The Philosophy of Jesus* and *The Life and Morals of Jesus* in four languages, often look askance when they see all references to miracles, supernature, or revelation disappear. They might also be fascinated to notice what and how much survived the Jeffersonian scissors.

Today some historians and film-makers are trying to cut him down because he held slaves or was an imperfect fighter for liberty or whatever else he gets accused of by a generation that thinks it can grow if it can diminish the greats who went before. But that cutting-down is not what some believers had against Jefferson, so much as his cutting out, with major parts of the gospels left on the cutting-room floor.

To many of the pious in Jefferson's own day, whether on grounds that mixed politics and religion—most of the pious Federalists saw him undercutting legally established, privileged, and tax-paid religion—or on purely religious grounds, the third president was abhorrent. The first historian of American religion, Robert Baird, called Jefferson "the arch-infidel." He knew that Jefferson had his own ideas about religion, Christianity, the gospels, and Jesus, and that these views conflicted with what almost all the churches taught.

Jefferson in the eyes of his enemies was both infidel and atheist. They were wrong on both counts. Jefferson was not "infidel," which means "of unfaith," but he had a different faith. He was not an "a-theist," which means "without a God," but, as noted, a Deist, who had a different concept of God, one that was characteristic of many Anglo-American intellectual figures of the Enlightenment.

Some of the Enlightened, especially in France, were indeed infidel and atheist. But in England and the colonies, soon the United States, they were reverent, respectful, often responsible clerical and lay leaders in newer fangled versions of Protestantism or in churchlike creations of their own. The Enlightened, who had great influence in the age of the Declaration of Independence, the Constitution, and most of the documents that charter our republic, believed that this republic had to rely upon virtuous and moral citizens, and that religion was a major grounding for, or instrument of, virtue and morality. They believed that one could not base laws upon supernatural revelations, as in the Bible, since citizens could not agree on which revelations were divine, or how to interpret them, or what to do about those who could believe in none of them. So they contended that virtues, morals, and religion could come from "Nature's God," revealed in the mind, conscience, and moral sense of reasonable people.

This belief did not induce them to disrespect scriptures. It did tempt them, as the reader will see in Eugene R. Sheridan's essay, to respect only certain parts of the Bible. They regarded themselves as free to excise and preserve these, while leaving other parts in cuttings on the floor.

The eighteenth century's religion of Enlightenment did not survive as a community. You will not find it among the hundreds of options that, along with newcoming faiths, did survive these two centuries. But you will find evidences of it in the individual writings of philosophers and politicians through the American centuries—and seldom as clearly set forth as by Thomas Jefferson.

— MARTIN E. MARTY
University of Chicago

The author of this essay, the late Eugene R. Sheridan, was a distinguished editor and historian. His authoritative essay is regarded by Jefferson scholars as one of the best treatments of its subject and originally appeared as the introduction to *Jefferson's Extracts from the Gospels: "The Philosophy of Jesus" and "The Life and Morals of Jesus,"* a volume in the second series of *The Papers of Thomas Jefferson,* published by the Princeton University Press. Permission to reprint this essay is gratefully acknowledged.

A few editorial changes have been made to the original text, mainly relating to the Jefferson documents referred to. Originally, the author quoted Jefferson's letters and other documents from manuscript and cited them by date only. For the convenience of the reader, a printed version of the document, if any is available, has been cited in the appropriate footnote. The reader is advised that the manuscript texts given by Mr. Sheridan may vary slightly from those in printed editions. In addition, a few of the footnote references have been updated.

Descent from the Cross *by Frans Floris (1516–1570), oil on wood, owned by Jefferson. (Thomas Jefferson Memorial Foundation, Inc.)*

"*F*IX REASON FIRMLY in her seat, and call to her tribunal every fact, every opinion," Thomas Jefferson advised one of his nephews in the course of a disquisition on religious education. "Question with boldness even the existence of a god; because, if there be one, he must more approve the homage of reason, than that of blindfolded fear."[1] This critical attitude, typical of the Age of Enlightenment, characterized Jefferson's approach to religion, as to all other problems, from his youth. But unlike many other adherents of the Enlightenment, especially those in France, Jefferson's rationalism led him ultimately to an affirmation of faith rather than a rejection of religious belief.

Jefferson's rational religion was perhaps nowhere better expressed than in his two compilations of extracts from the New Testament—"The Philosophy of Jesus" (1804) and "The Life and Morals of Jesus" (1819-1820?). Since coming to public attention in the mid-nineteenth century, these efforts by Jefferson to ascertain the authentic acts and teachings of Jesus have been surrounded by much confusion.[2] Some scholars have confused "The Philosophy of Jesus" with "The Life and Morals of Jesus," a few even failing to realize that they are two distinct works. Others have accepted uncritically the subtitle of "The Philosophy of Jesus," concluding that Jefferson prepared it for the use of the Indians. And still others have assumed that Jefferson produced both compilations strictly for his personal edification, thereby dismissing evidence which suggests that the composition of "The Philosophy of Jesus" was motivated in part by his apprehensions over the future of republicanism in the United States.[3] Most of this confusion stems from the unfortunate disappearance of Jefferson's first biblical compilation. A careful reconstruction of the text of "The Philosophy of Jesus" and the collection of Jefferson's papers at one place[4] now make it possible to place that manuscript and "The Life and Morals of Jesus" in their proper historical context by tracing the development of Jefferson's religious attitudes, describing the genesis of both documents, and discussing their significance in the evolution of his religious beliefs.

⇥ **I** ⇤

Jefferson's religion has long fascinated and vexed students of his career. Always reticent about his private life, Jefferson was especially reluctant to reveal his religious beliefs. Indeed, so firmly was he convinced that religion was essentially a private affair between each person and his god that he studiously avoided religious discussions even with members of his own family lest he have undue influence upon their views.[5] "Say nothing of my religion," he admonished a correspondent who was seeking information on his personal beliefs for a biographical sketch. "It is known to my god and myself alone."[6] Although Jefferson did in fact discuss his religious beliefs in a few letters written late in life, before then he rarely touched on this subject in his surviving correspondence. Nevertheless, enough evidence has survived to make possible a reliable reconstruction of the main lines of his religious development before he became president.

Jefferson came of age at a critical point in the religious history of the Western world. By the middle of the eighteenth century the Enlightenment was in full swing in Europe and America. The Enlightenment was a highly complex movement that went through several different stages of development and varied in emphasis and strength from country to country, but in general it represented a decisive shift, at least among the educated elite, from a predominantly theological to a fundamentally secular world view. Inspired by the successes of the Scientific Revolution and weary of a long series of inclusive religious wars and doctrinal disputes between Catholics and Protestants, enlightened thinkers scorned metaphysical and theological speculation as useless and concentrated instead on the rational investigation of nature and society, making their main goal the improvement of man's lot in this life rather than the preparation of souls for salvation in a life to come. The rationalistic spirit that animated the Enlightenment inevitably brought it into conflict with organized Christianity, whose emphasis on the value of supernatural revelation, tradition, and ecclesiastical authority was rejected by those who insisted that religion, like all other institutions, had to be justified instead on the twin grounds of reasonableness and social utility. The Enlightenment's demand for the rationalization and demystification of religion evoked a variety of responses. Latitudinarians sought to prove the reasonableness of Christianity, Deists preached the sufficiency of natural religion, and skeptics and atheists rejected religion as superstition—and these beliefs all coexisted in many quarters with a continued defense of Christian orthodoxy on traditional grounds. The rationalistic critique of Christianity was far less prominent in the American Enlightenment than in its European counterpart owing to the high degree of religious toleration that existed in the British colonies. In the case of Jefferson, however, who in this respect was more closely attuned to the European Enlightenment than most of his American contemporaries, the tension between the spirit of critical analysis and the tenets of traditional Christianity was the central theme of his religious history.

The precise details and chronology are still somewhat obscure, but it seems clear that at some point during the 1760s Jefferson experienced a religious crisis in the course of which he rejected his ancestral Anglican creed and embraced instead a vaguely defined natural religion. This religious transformation was apparently caused by Jefferson's inability "from a very early part of my life" to accept the central Christian doctrine of the Trinity owing to the "difficulty of reconciling the ideas of Unity and Trinity" in the godhead.[7] His rationalism led him, in the words of a contemporary Virginian, to repudiate "as falsehoods things unsusceptible of strict demonstration."[8] Having rejected the dogma of the Trinity as a logical absurdity that could not be reconciled with human reason, Jefferson then subjected the rest of Christianity to the test of rational analysis and concluded that its basic doctrines were simply unacceptable to an enlightened man living in the eighteenth century. "The person who becomes sponsor for a child, according to the ritual of the church in which I was educated," he later explained in declining a French friend's request that he serve as godfather to his son, "makes a solemn profession, before god and the world, of faith in articles, which I had never sense enough to comprehend, and it has always appeared to me that comprehension must precede assent."[9]

The process by which Jefferson came to reject the validity of Christianity can be traced in part through an analysis of the passages from the works of Henry St. John, Viscount Bolingbroke, the rakish Tory political leader and man of letters, that Jefferson laboriously entered into his literary commonplace book, a notebook consisting of extracts from the writings of various ancient and modern dramatists, philosophers, and poets, compiled largely in the 1760s and early 1770s.[10] Bolingbroke's philosophical writings, which are a veritable summa of rationalistic criticisms of revealed religion, constitute by far the longest single entry in the literary commonplace book, running to almost sixty pages in manuscript, and are the only works therein that deal specifically with the subject of Christianity. It is therefore highly significant that Jefferson turned to these writings during what was evidently a period of intellectual turmoil in his youth, and it is almost certain, in view of his later remarks on religion, that the extracts he made from them reflect his own views. These selections, some of which he copied verbatim and others of which he paraphrased, suggest that Jefferson, like Bolingbroke, felt obliged to reject as contrary to human reason the basic foundations of Christianity. Thus, the Bible was not the inspired word of God because, as Bolingbroke argued, inspiration itself is a concept that cannot be proved by evidence "such as no reasonable man can refuse to admit" and also because the scriptures contain many "gross defects and palpable falsehoods ... such as no man who acknowledges a supreme all-perfect being can believe to be his word."[11] The Christian scheme of divine revelation was likewise objectionable inasmuch as it postulated that for centuries the one true God had restricted knowledge of himself to a small nation on the eastern rim of the Mediterranean while leaving the rest of the world in a spiritual void—"it is impossible to conceive, on grounds of human reason, to what purpose a divine economy, relative to the coming of Christ, should have confined the knowledge of the true god to the Jews, and have left the rest of mankind without god in the world."[12] No less absurd were the Christian plan of redemption and the doctrine of the fall of man upon which it was predicated. In regard to the latter, it was "in all circumstances, absolutely irreconcilable to every idea we can frame of wisdom, justice, and goodness, to say nothing of the dignity of the supreme being"; and as for the former, it was simply inconceivable that a just God "sent his only begotten son, who had not offended him, to be sacrificed by men, who had offended him, that he might expiate their sins, and satisfy his own anger."[13] In fact, Bolingbroke decided, God had not sent his son to redeem the world because Jesus was not divine. The miracles Jesus supposedly worked "were equivocal at best, such as credulous superstitious persons, and none else, believed, such as were frequently and universally imposed by the first fathers of the Christian church, and as are so still by their successors, wherever ignorance or superstition abound"; he failed to reveal "an entire body of ethics, proved to be the law of nature from principles of reason, and reaching all the duties of life"; and the history of the development of Christian doctrine after his death indicated that the "system of belief and practise" he taught were not "complete and perfect, forcing one to assume that the son of god, who was sent by the father to make a new covenant with mankind, and to establish a new kingdom on the ruins of paganism, executed his commission imperfectly."[14] Finally, Bolingbroke was repelled by the nature of the god who was revealed in the Bible. In the Old Testament this deity was "partial, unjust, and cruel; delights in blood, commands assassinations, massacres[,] and even exterminations of people," while in the New Testament he "elects some of his creatures to salvation, and predestinates others to damnation, even in the womb of their mothers."[15] In sum, traditional Christianity was unacceptable to a rational man because its fundamental doctrines were basically mysteries that could not be comprehended by human reason, and "No man can believe he knoweth not what nor why."[16]

It is evident from random comments in Jefferson's writings that these selections from Bolingbroke's works accurately reflect his own considered opinion of Christianity before the late 1790s. For example, the Bible, far from being the revealed word of God, was for Jefferson merely a human "History" that he advised one of his nephews to read "as you would read Livy or Tacitus."[17] Instead of being the son of God, Jesus was only "a man, of illegitimate birth, of a benevolent heart, enthusiastic mind, who set out without pretensions to divinity, ended in believing them, and was punished capitally for sedition by being gibbetted according to the Roman law."[18] Rather than an inspiring chapter in the development of mankind, Jefferson saw in the history of Christianity a gloomy chronicle of successive "corruptions" of its pristine "Purity" and a series of misguided efforts to impose doctrinal uniformity upon the world, which had stifled free thought, led "Millions of innocent men, women, and children" to be "burnt, tortured, fined, imprisoned," and made "one half the world fools, and the other half hypocrites."[19] In fact, Jefferson confided to an English correspondent on the eve of the French Revolution, in one of his harshest criticisms of orthodox Christianity, most forms of Christian worship were nothing less than "demonism."[20]

As in the case of many other enlightened eighteenth-century thinkers, the young Jefferson turned to natural religion after discarding his inherited Christian faith. Calvin "was indeed an Atheist, which I can never be," Jefferson confided late in life to John Adams, thereby revealing the limits of his religious skepticism, "or rather his religion was Daemonism. If ever man worshipped a false god, he did."[21] For Jefferson, human reason, not supernatural revelation or ecclesiastical authority, henceforth became the sole arbiter of religious truth. Thus, through rational investigation he came to believe in a supreme being who created the universe and continued to sustain it by means of fixed, mathematically precise natural laws—"the Creator and benevolent

FIGURE I. *John Adams (Courtesy of Boston Athenæum)*

governor of the world."[22] Disdaining miraculous interventions in human affairs, this benevolent being revealed himself to all men at all times and in all places through the natural wonders of the created universe and was therefore infinitely superior to the arbitrary, jealous, mysterious, and vindictive deity that Jefferson perceived in the Old and New Testaments. "The missionary of supernatural religion appeals to the testimony of men he never knew, and of whom the infidel he labors to convert never heard, for the truth of those extraordinary events which prove the revelation he preaches ...," Jefferson quoted approvingly from Bolingbroke. "But the missionary of natural religion can appeal at all times, and every where, to present and immediate evidence, to the testimony of sense and intellect, for the truth of those miracles which he brings in proof: the constitution of the mundane system being in a very proper sense an aggregate of miracles."[23]

In addition to substituting the god of nature for the god of revelation, Jefferson also found a new basis for morality to replace the traditional spiritual sanctions of Christianity. Under the influence of the writings of the Scottish philosopher Henry Home, Lord Kames, Jefferson concluded that God had endowed each person with an innate faculty for distinguishing right from wrong, known as the moral sense. The moral sense performed this function, he believed, by making virtue pleasing and vice displeasing to men, nature having "implanted in our breasts a love of others, a sense of duty to them, a moral instinct in short, which prompts us irresistibly to feel and succour their distresses."[24] At the same time, by directing men to differentiate between good and evil on the basis of social utility, the moral standards prescribed by this faculty varied from age to age and culture to culture—a species of relativism Jefferson accepted with equanimity. The moral sense did not work automatically, however. It had to be instructed by education and example to incline a person toward right conduct. In order therefore to cultivate and nurture his own moral sense, Jefferson as a young man turned to the ethical precepts of the classical Epicurean and Stoic philosophers, thereby seeking to achieve the good life as defined by the former through the stern self-discipline enjoined by the latter. For at that time he wholeheartedly agreed with the contention of his intellectual mentor Bolingbroke that a "system of ethics ... collected from the writings of ancient heathen moralists of Tully, of Seneca, of Epictetus, and others, would be more full, more entire, more coherent, and more clearly deduced from unquestionable principles of knowledge" than that taught in the New Testament by Jesus of Nazareth—a judgment Jefferson radically revised during his administration as president.[25]

Jefferson's early rejection of traditional Christian doctrine and adoption of natural religion left him with a lifelong belief in the need for freedom of thought and the primacy of morality over dogma in religious affairs. Each person, he decided, had a natural right to worship—or not to worship—God as he pleased. Since the very essence of religion was the free assent of the human mind to what it deemed to be God's truth, no one could be forced to believe what his intellect rejected, for coercion produced hypocrisy rather than conviction and was thus an affront to God and man alike. Everyone, therefore, must be free to decide for himself the truth or falsity of the claims of particular religions—hence the fervor with which Jefferson threw himself into the struggle during the American Revolution to disestablish the Anglican Church in Virginia.[26] By the same token, Jefferson welcomed the diversity of religious views that freedom of inquiry entailed. Although he personally rejected supernatural revelation and church authority as valid sources of religious truth, his deep commitment to freedom of conscience led him to respect the opinions of those who did accept them. For in regard to religion what ultimately mattered to him was the quality of a person's life, not the truth of the doctrines in which he believed or the nature of the church to which he belonged. In New York and Pennsylvania, he wrote in *Notes on Virginia*, "Religion is well supported; of various kinds, indeed, but all good enough; all sufficient to preserve peace and good order."[27] His manner of expression in this case was unusually harsh, and elsewhere he expressed the same sentiment in milder terms. But the main point is clear: the best measure of the efficacy of any religion is the character of the moral standards it instills in its adherents rather than the substance of the theological doctrines it teaches. Whereas in his opinion dogma dealt with matters that were beyond human understanding and that historically had provoked bitter strife, morality regulated human relations in the social world to which men had been destined by nature, and had the potential to generate harmony in society—a key element in the Jeffersonian hierarchy of values. "Reading, reflection and time have convinced me," he noted shortly after his retirement from the presidency, expressing a long-held view, "that the interests of society require the observation of those moral precepts only in which all religions agree, (for all forbid us to murder, steal, plunder, or bear false witness) and that we should not intermeddle with the particular dogmas in which all religions differ, and which are totally unconnected with morality."[28] Thus Jefferson's religion was basically moralistic in emphasis, as befitted one whose controlling purpose in life was the improvement of man and society in this world rather than the next.

Despite the leading role Jefferson played in the campaign to separate church and state in Virginia, his own religious views did not become a major public issue until the time of the bitter party conflict between Federalists and Republicans in the late 1790s. After leveling sporadic allegations of infidelity against Jefferson beginning as early as the election of 1796,[29] Federalist leaders and their clerical supporters in New England and the middle states made this theme the centerpiece of a powerful propaganda offensive that was designed to blacken his character and destroy his electoral support during the presidential campaign of 1800. As Jefferson's prospects for winning the presidency in 1800 increased, some Federalists, desperately eager to retain control of the executive branch of government, unleashed a frenzied barrage of vituperative attacks upon his personal character and public record. They poured scorn on him for his alleged cowardice as governor of Virginia. They heaped ridicule on him as an unworldly philosopher and scientist who was unfit to conduct weighty affairs of state. They denounced the imprudent letter to his Italian friend Philip Mazzei in which he suggested that Washington was an apostate to revolutionary principles. They charged that he was an undiscriminating Francophile whose inordinate sympathy for the French Revolution would bring the worst excesses of Jacobinism to the United States. They warned that he was an enemy of the federal Constitution who wanted to undo the work of the Philadelphia Convention. And they argued that he was a narrow-minded agrarian who was irrationally hostile to the interests of commerce and industry. But most of all the Federalists and their ministerial allies arraigned Jefferson before the bar of public opinion as an unbeliever who was unworthy to serve as chief magistrate of a Christian nation.[30]

Since Jefferson had carefully concealed his private religious views from the public, his critics seized upon selected passages from *Notes on Virginia,* his first and only published book, to prove their contention that he was fundamentally hostile to religion. Hence they charged that his refusal to admit that a "universal deluge" was a sufficient explanation for the presence of shells high atop the Andes was a veiled attack upon the account of the flooding of the world in Genesis, which made the Virginia leader a party to that "war upon revelation [in which] infidels have levelled their batteries against the miraculous *facts* of the scripture: well knowing that if its historical truth can be overturned, there is an end to its claim of inspiration."[31] They pointed to his "suggestion" that blacks might have been originally created as a distinct race as proof of his disbelief in the biblical account of the creation of man and argued that if Jefferson's hypothesis were correct it would mean that "the history of the Bible, which knows of but one [race], is a string of falsehoods from the book of Genesis to that of Revelation; and the whole system of redemption, predicated on the unity of the human race, is a cruel fiction."[32] They construed his remark that farmers were the chosen people of God "if ever he had a chosen people" to signify that he rejected the providential role of the Jews in the Christian scheme of salvation history, and they contended that his proposal not to teach the Bible to young children indicated his opposition to religious education in general.[33] But worst of all, in the opinion of Jefferson's critics, was his argument that the state should refrain from interfering with religion because, among other things, "it does me no injury for my neighbor to say there are twenty gods or no god. It neither picks my pocket nor breaks my leg."[34] Instead of indicating Jefferson's tolerance for divergent religious points of view, they insisted that at the very least this statement revealed a disturbing indifference to religion that could have profoundly dangerous social consequences. "Let my neighbor once persuade himself that there is no God," a New York minister warned, "and he will soon pick my pocket, and break not only my *leg* but my *neck*. If there be no God, there is no law, no future account; government then is the ordinance of man only, and we cannot be subject for conscience sake."[35]

In the light of this evidence, Jefferson's opponents triumphantly proclaimed, the conclusion was clear. Jefferson was an atheist, an infidel, or at best a deist (in their zeal to undermine his popular support his critics frequently sacrificed analytical rigor to rhetorical effect) who was hostile to Christianity and therefore unworthy to serve in the highest office possible for the American people to bestow upon a fellow citizen. Elect Jefferson to the presidency, they warned, and dire consequences would ensue for the fledgling republic. His victory would arouse the wrath of God himself, "destroy religion, introduce immorality ... loosen all the bonds of society," and undermine the standing of the United States among the nations of the world. "Can serious and reflecting men look about them and doubt," asked "A Christian Federalist," conjuring up an awful vision of the apocalypse that was bound to result from the triumph of the allegedly irreligious Republican leader, "that if Jefferson is elected, and the Jacobins get into authority, that those morals which protect our lives from the knife of the assassin—which guard the chastity of our wives and daughters from seduction and violence—defend our property from plunder and devastation, and shield our religion from contempt and profanation, will not be trampled upon and exploded."[36]

The object of this relentless wave of criticism steadfastly refused to reply to his critics during the election of 1800, believing as a matter of principle that he was accountable to God alone for his religious convictions and realizing as a practical matter that nothing he could say would silence his detractors. As a result, charges that he was an irreligious enemy of Christianity plagued Jefferson throughout his administration as president and especially during his first term. As his popularity rose and as the power of the Republican party increased throughout the Union, the Federalists and their supporters among the clergy found that the accusation of infidelity was one of the few weapons they could still use against him with some hope of success. Moreover, although later attacks on Jefferson's views of religion never again reached the intensity of those in 1800, the technique of criticism, at least on the level of published discourse, continued to focus on his *Notes on Virginia*. For example, a New York minister, known more familiarly as the author of a famous Yuletide poem, published a pamphlet during the election of 1804 in which he examined the same parts of this book and arrived at the same conclusion as his predecessors four years before. "But can any person who believes the testimony of his senses and reason," he asked, "deny that the book which offers a theory of the earth contrary to the scripture account of creation; which denies the possibility of a universal deluge; which considers the Bible history as no better than ordinary tradition; which extols Voltaire and the French Encyclopediests, the imps who have inspired all the wickedness with which the world has of late years been infested; which says that the natives of America are older than those of Asia, though scripture says that the world was peopled from one pair, placed in Asia; which considers it as a doubtful matter whether the blacks be really men, or only an intermediate grade between us and the brutes; and which esteems all religions 'good enough'; can he deny that this book is an instrument of infidelity?"[37]

By that time, however, Jefferson had in fact responded to accusations that he was irreligious and hostile to Christianity, though, characteristically, he did so privately rather than publicly.

II

The charges of infidelity that were hurled against Jefferson by his Federalist and clerical adversaries set in motion a train of events that led him to compose his famous "Syllabus ... of the merit of the doctrines of Jesus" in 1803 and its less well known successor, "The Philosophy of Jesus," in the following year. In compiling these two works, Jefferson was motivated by more than just a simple wish to rebut those who were assailing his character on religious grounds. He was also responding to another problem that was of deep concern to him: how to guarantee the perpetuation of republican government in the United States at a time when, as it seemed to him, political factionalism and social disharmony were threatening to undermine its basic foundations. Jefferson's solution to this problem was an effort to foster the social harmony that he considered essential for the survival of America's republican experiment by formulating a moralistic version of Christianity on which all men of good will could agree. Thus, in addition to demonstrating to a select group of relatives and friends that he was indeed a good Christian according to his own lights, Jefferson also wrote the "Syllabus" and compiled "The Philosophy of Jesus" to set forth a demystified form of Christianity that he deemed appropriate for a society that had chosen to live according to republican principles. Typically, he went to great lengths to present that version of Christianity to his countrymen through the medium of an author other than himself.

Jefferson's apprehensions over the future of republicanism in the United States grew markedly in the 1790s as political life in the new nation was polarized by the rise of two national parties with sharply opposing principles and policies. As the country divided along Republican and Federalist lines, Jefferson became increasingly convinced that the very future of popular government in America was the central issue at stake between the two parties. The institutions of the

Hamiltonian fiscal system, the adoption of a foreign policy that seemingly appeased aristocratic Britain while affronting republican France, the employment of military force in Pennsylvania to suppress popular discontent, the creation of a large standing army during the XYZ crisis, and the use of the Sedition Act to silence Republican political criticism of the Adams administration—these things portended nothing less to Jefferson than a settled Federalist design to create a monarchical government in the United States.[38] Nor was this a passing mood. Jefferson remained convinced until the end of his life that only the triumph of the Republican party in 1800 had prevented the Federalists from carrying out this nefarious design and thereby assured the continuance of America's experiment in republicanism. Just a few months before his death he pointed with pride to his leadership of the Republican cause during the bitter party battles of the 1790s as the most important public service he had ever rendered the nation, and he claimed that the "spirits of the people were so much rendered desperate by the X.Y.Z. imposture, and other stratagems and machinations," that if it had not been for his own efforts and those of his supporters "they would have sunk into apathy and monarchy, as the only form of government which could maintain itself."[39]

At the same time that Jefferson became apprehensive over putative Federalist threats to the survival of republican government in the new nation, he repeatedly lamented that political differences between adherents of the two parties were becoming so acrimonious that they were undermining the social harmony and tolerance he thought essential for a republic. Differences of opinion over political issues were only to be expected in a free government and might even lead to sharp debate between the contending sides. But if such disputes became so intense as to destroy social harmony, there would be no possibility of compromise to the satisfaction of all the parties involved. Society would then become divided into hostile classes and interests, with each one striving to advance its goals at the expense of the others instead of all cooperating together harmoniously to achieve the public good. "The passions are too high at present, to be cooled in our day," he wrote to a southern supporter soon after taking office as vice-president, in a frank revelation of his fear of the corrosive impact of partisan strife on social harmony. "You and I have seen warm debates and high political passions. But gentlemen of different politics would then speak to each other and separate the business of the Senate from that of society. It is not so now. Men who have been intimate all their lives, cross the streets to avoid meeting, and turn their heads another way, lest they should be obliged to touch their hats. This may do for young men with whom passion is enjoyment. But it is affecting to peaceable minds."[40] Since Jefferson believed that the preservation of harmonious social relations was to a large extent a matter of personal morality and character, it is not surprising that as the eighteenth century drew to a close he began to be interested in a moral system that would be more efficacious for this purpose than that offered by the classical philosophers who had hitherto been his main ethical guides.

Jefferson's growing concern during the 1790s with the need to preserve social harmony in the midst of sharp partisan conflicts coincided with a significant shift in his personal attitude toward Christianity. Ironically, at the very time public attacks on him as an enemy of Christianity were mounting, Jefferson was in the process of adopting a much more sympathetic view of that religion than he had previously entertained. This change came about largely as a result of the influence of Dr. Joseph Priestley's *An History of the Corruptions of Christianity*, a two-volume work that Jefferson acquired and read sometime after 1793. Priestley, a noted English chemist and Unitarian theologian, set forth a highly demythologized version of Christianity in these tomes, which so impressed Jefferson that he adopted key parts of it and later described the work itself as the "groundwork of my view of this subject" and as one of the bases "of my own faith."[41] The English champion of Unitarianism, who become one of Jefferson's friends after moving to the United States in 1794 to escape political persecution in his native land, argued that Christianity was originally a simple religion that had been corrupted by the early church in a misguided effort to make it intellectually respectable to pagans and by later churchmen for the less edifying purpose of increasing their power over the laity. The essence of true Christianity, Priestley insisted, could be summed up in a few plain propositions. There was but one God, and He had given Jesus the special mission of revealing His true nature to the world and of teaching men how to lead virtuous lives on earth so that they would be rewarded rather than punished in the life to come. Jesus was not a member of the godhead, nor did he ever claim to be. Nevertheless, God signified his approval of Jesus' teachings by enabling him to perform miracles and to rise from the dead, thereby making him the greatest moral teacher who had ever lived. As a result, mankind was obliged to worship the one true God and to follow the moral teachings of Jesus. Virtually everything else in orthodox Christianity—doctrines like the Trinity, the atonement, and original sin, as well as devotional practices like the veneration of relics and saints—was a corruption of the primitive purity of the Christian message and had to be discarded so as to restore Christianity to its pristine simplicity and thus make it acceptable to modern men, who were otherwise inclined to reject it as a mass of superstitions.[42]

Priestley's work made a deep and lasting impression on Jefferson. It convinced him that the early Christians had a Unitarian concept of God and that therefore one like himself could be a true Christian without being a Trinitarian. It persuaded him that Jesus had never laid claim to divinity, which to him made Jesus more credible as a great moral teacher. It increased his appreciation of Christian morality by demonstrating to his satisfaction that the dogmas that had led him to reject the validity of Christianity in his youth were in fact perversions of the primitive Christian message rather than integral parts of it.[43] Rejecting Priestley's Socialism, he still refused to entertain the possibility that Jesus had performed miracles or risen from the dead because these actions contravened what he understood to be the unvarying character of the laws of nature. Otherwise, he fully accepted Priestley's contention that true Christianity was basically a simple religion whose original emphasis on the unity of God and the primacy of morality over dogma had been perverted through the course of history by the development of metaphysical and theological doctrines no human mind could understand and by the introduction of forms of worship no rational man could practice without degrading himself. Unlike his English intellectual mentor, however, Jefferson most frequently attributed these corruptions to the sinister machinations of the clergy, who, he believed, deliberately sought to make religion as mysterious as possible in order to render themselves indispensable to the people over whom they presumed to exercise spiritual authority. "The mild and simple principles of the Christian philosophy," he argued shortly after being sworn in as president for the first time, "would produce too much calm, too much regularity of good, to extract from it's disciples a support for a numerous priesthood, were they not to sophisticate it, ramify it, split it into hairs, and twist it's texts till they cover the divine morality of it's author with mysteries, and require a priesthood to explain them."[44] Jefferson had long suspected that primitive Christianity had been corrupted in the course of history, but it remained for Priestley to enable him to work out the full implications of this insight.[45] Thus, by presenting him with a demystified form of Christianity that compared with his rationalistic world view, Priestley made it possible for Jefferson to regard himself as a genuine Christian and launched him on the quest for the authentic teachings of Jesus that was to lead in time to the "Syllabus" and "The Philosophy of Jesus."

As Jefferson's view of Christianity was changing under the impact of the writings of Dr. Priestley, he began to consider the relationship between republicanism and Christianity under the influence of that perennial gadfly, Dr. Benjamin Rush. Jefferson first became friendly with the noted Philadelphia physician and social reformer during the Revolution, when as fellow members of the Continental Congress, they had worked together to advance the twin causes of American independence and union. Although both men remained convinced

FIGURE 2. *Joseph Priestley (Courtesy of Dickinson College Special Collections)*

FIGURE 3. *Benjamin Rush (Courtesy of Mütter Museum, College of Physicians of Philadelphia)*

republicans, their paths had later diverged owing to their sharply differing perceptions of the ultimate significance of America's republican destiny. Whereas the philosophically rationalistic Jefferson regarded republicanism as basically a secular movement that was designed to improve humanity and society by restoring the natural rights of man and expanding the scope of self-government, the theologically universalist Rush considered it as essentially a religious movement that was part of a divine plan to bring about the kingdom of God on earth by freeing mankind from the burden of royal and ecclesiastical oppression through the spread of the principles of human equality and Christian charity.[46] Thus Rush believed that Christianity and republicanism, far from being antithetical, actually stood in a symbiotic relationship with each other. The progress of both was necessary to achieve the millennium to which he looked forward. "Republican forms of government are the best repositories of the gospel," he declared in 1791. "I therefore suppose they are intended as preludes to a glorious manifestation of its power and influence upon the hearts of men."[47] Convinced that Jefferson's secular outlook on life was blinding him to the most vital dimension of America's republican experiment, the zealous Rush characteristically took it upon himself to set forth his alternative view of the matter to his erring Virginia friend.

Rush began to carry out his self-appointed mission after Jefferson emerged from retirement and returned to Philadelphia in 1797 to serve as vice-president. During the next several years the two men discussed the subject of Christianity in a series of conversations, which, Jefferson later recalled, "served as an Anodyne to the afflictions of the crisis through which our country was then labouring."[48] In view of Jefferson's reluctance to discuss his religious beliefs, it seems plausible to assume that it was Rush who initiated these talks. At any rate, in the course of the conversations Jefferson denied Federalist charges that he was hostile to Christianity and indicated that although he accepted certain Christian doctrines he did not believe in the divinity of Jesus.[49] Rush welcomed these professions of support for Christianity, all the more so since he had suspected Jefferson of infidelity, but he was disappointed by Jefferson's unwillingness to go even further and acknowledge that Christ was divine. In order to correct this deficiency Rush urged Jefferson to read William Paley's *A View of the Evidences of Christianity*, a widely used handbook of orthodox criticisms of Deism by a noted English moralist and theologian, and extracted a promise from him to provide a written statement on his religious beliefs for Rush's perusal. But Jefferson found himself unable at this time to state his view of Christianity in a way that would satisfy Rush, and therefore he hesitated to fulfill his pledge.[50]

Personal conversation having failed to achieve the desired objective, the indefatigable Rush next resorted to epistolary persuasion. As the presidential campaign of 1800 progressed and the prospect of a Republican electoral triumph grew more probable, he addressed two important letters to Jefferson at Monticello, stressing the theme that Christianity and republicanism were organically related. Writing in August, Rush first reminded Jefferson of his promised statement on religion and then, in an obvious effort to instruct him as to the real significance of America's republican experiment, emphasized that true Christianity was the firmest guarantee for the success of republican government. "I have always considered Christianity as the *strong ground* of Republicanism," he observed to the man he now thought was most likely to become the nation's next chief magistrate: "Its spirit is opposed, not only to the Splendor, but even to the very forms of monarchy, and many of its precepts have for their Objects republican liberty and equality, as well as simplicity, integrity, and Œconomy in government. It is only necessary for Republicanism to ally itself to the christian Religion, to overturn all the corrupted political and religious institutions in the world."[51]

At first Jefferson was unresponsive to Rush's exposition of the interrelationship between republicanism and Christianity. In replying to his Philadelphia correspondent he firmly maintained that his attitude toward Christianity would "displease neither the rational Christian or Deist; and would reconcile many to a character they have too hastily rejected." Nevertheless, he pleaded that he still needed more time to produce a satisfactory statement of his religious creed. Then, ignoring the main point of Rush's letter, he lashed out at his clerical tormentors, charging that they were secretly bent upon making Christianity the legally established religion of the United States.[52] Fearing that the entire thrust of his argument had been misunderstood, Rush hastened to reassure Jefferson that an established church was the farthest thing from his mind. It was not through a union of church and state that Christianity would advance the cause of republicanism, Rush wrote in October, since that would only corrupt religion and politics alike. Rather, this advancement would come about through the voluntary acceptance by a free people of the "simple doctrines and precepts of Christianity," doctrines and precepts which, he readily admitted, had been "dishonoured by being mixed with human follies and crimes by the corrupted Churches of Europe," but which, when purged of centuries of accumulated dross and restored to their primitive simplicity, would, he was certain, eventually lead to the spread of true Christianity and republican forms of government throughout the globe.[53]

Although Jefferson did not reply to Rush's second letter, in the end the Philadelphian's proselytizing efforts enjoyed a limited success. By forcing Jefferson to confront the issue of the relationship between Christianity and republicanism at a time when his attitude toward the former was undergoing a significant change, Rush was instrumental in inducing him to take a view of the subject that was somewhat in accord with his own. To be sure, Jefferson always remained immune to Rush's extravagant millennial hopes, and he refused to follow him in accepting such fundamental Christian doctrines as the divinity of Jesus. But he did decide that Christian morality could serve as one of the basic foundations of the country's republican experiments by promoting the social harmony among the citizenry that he considered essential for the survival of the republic. The "Christian religion," he told one of his New England supporters soon after taking over the reins of government from John Adams, "when divested of the rages in which [the clergy] have enveloped it, is a religion of all others most friendly to liberty, science and the freest expansions of the human mind."[54] It would be wrong to attribute Jefferson's new appreciation of the role of Christian morality in a republican society exclusively to Rush's influence, but it would also be unfair to underestimate the Philadelphia doctor's role in its development.

Thus as Jefferson began his first term as president several factors had converged to arouse his interest in ascertaining the true teachings of Jesus. Public criticism of his alleged atheism and infidelity had caused him to reexamine his attitude toward Christianity. The fierce party conflicts of the 1790s had disrupted the social harmony he valued as one of the main pillars of republicanism and made him sensitive to the need for a more effective system of ethical principles to inform the moral sense of the new nation than the one provided by his classical Epicurean and Stoic guides. The writings of Dr. Priestley had offered him a version of Christianity that was well suited to his rationalistic frame of mind. And his exchanges with Dr. Rush had heightened his awareness of the social utility of Christian morality. Yet for a number of reasons two more years were to pass before he openly formed these disparate elements into a coherent system. To begin with, his electoral victory over John Adams convinced him that the specter of monarchical government in the United States had been banished and temporarily soothed his fears about the threat posed to social harmony by severe partisan conflicts. Accordingly, by adopting a conciliatory policy toward the defeated Federalists, he hoped to entice the bulk of their followers to enlist under the Republican banner, and by scrupulously respecting the right of all citizens to religious freedom, he sought to disarm those who claimed that he was an enemy of Christianity.[55] In addition, he still had not found a way of reconciling his acceptance of Christian morality with his rejection of Christian dogma that might satisfy those who differed with him. Thus he had a further incentive for maintaining a discreet silence on the subject of his religious beliefs. As a result, it required the appearance of another timely work by Priestley, coupled with a revival of Jefferson's concern about preserving social harmony in the young republic and a sharp rise in public criticism of him on religious grounds, to impel him to produce a formal statement of his view of the Christian religion and to make his first compilation of passages from the New Testament.

The work by Priestley that had such a catalytic effect on Jefferson was an otherwise modest publication entitled *Socrates and Jesus Compared*. In this sixty-page pamphlet, published in Philadelphia early in 1803, Priestley sought to demonstrate that revealed religion was superior to natural religion by assessing the relative merits of the founder of Christianity and the man the Unitarian leader regarded as the crowning glory of ancient philosophy. Socrates and Jesus, Priestley argued, each had certain personal characteristics in common. Both were wise men who led temperate private lives. Both were virtuous men who strove to persuade other men to act virtuously. Both were religious men who submitted to a higher power. Both were poor men who shunned riches, and both were honest men who displayed great courage throughout their lives, especially in the face of death.[56] Yet, ultimately, their differences far outweighed their similarities. Jesus was a monotheist who taught humanity to worship the one true God, whereas Socrates was a polytheist who had no notion of the unity of God. Jesus emphasized that "great sanction of virtue,"[57] the doctrine of rewards and punishment in the life to come, whereas Socrates was uncertain whether there was life after death. Jesus stressed that piety consisted of inner reverence for God, and morality of obedience to his unchanging laws, whereas Socrates equated the former with the observance of frequently licentious public rituals and the latter with conformity to mutable human laws. Jesus, though less well educated than Socrates, exuded greater authority and dealt with more important subjects in his teachings, the primary object of which was "to inculcate a purer and more sublime morality respecting god and man than any heathen could have a just idea of."[58] Jesus was more forthright and fearless in denouncing all forms of vice; Socrates preferred to express his disapproval indirectly through ridicule and was regrettably deficient in opposing secular laxity. Jesus preached his moral doctrines for all mankind, reaching out to high and low, rich and poor, male and female alike, whereas Socrates confined his teachings to the upper classes, thus making Christian morality more useful to a republican society inasmuch as it was expressed in a "language suited to the equal nature, and equal rights of all men."[59] Finally, Jesus worked miracles and rose from the dead, thereby demonstrating that his teachings were specially approved by God, though he himself was only a man.[60] In Priestley's opinion there was only one way to explain why Jesus had purer notions of God, morality, and life after death than the better educated Athenian. "In comparing the characters, the moral instructions, and the whole of the history, of Socrates and Jesus," he concluded, "it is, I think, impossible not to be sensibly struck with the great advantage of revealed religion, such as that of the Jews and the christians, as enlightening and enlarging the minds of men, and imparting a superior excellence of character. This alone can account for the difference between Socrates and Jesus, and the disciples of each of them; but this one circumstance is abundantly sufficient for the purpose."[61]

Jefferson was immediately impressed by both the message and the methodology of *Socrates and Jesus*. He received a copy of the pamphlet from Priestley near the end of March 1803, just as he was about to leave Monticello for Washington, and read it with growing interest on his way back to the capital. Although he was unconvinced by Priestley's contention that the founder of Christianity had been divinely inspired and endowed with supernatural powers, he agreed wholeheartedly that "the moral precepts of Jesus … as taught by himself and freed from the corruptions of latter times" were unquestionably superior to any other system of morality and particularly appropriate for a republican society dedicated to the principles of liberty and equality.[62] He especially appreciated the way in which Priestley weighed the advantages of Christianity against the shortcomings of ancient philosophy without denigrating the genuine achievements of the classical philosophers, whom the president continued to admire. Indeed, Jefferson was so impressed by Priestley's use of the comparative method in *Socrates and Jesus* that he decided it would also be an excellent way for him to present his own unorthodox religious views. Thus, inspired by the example of Priestley's pamphlet, Jefferson quickly made two important and, for him, unprecedented decisions. He decided to reveal his view of the Christian religion to a small circle of relatives and friends in the form of a comparative analysis of the moral teachings of the classical philosophers, the Jews, and Jesus so as to convince them that he was not irreligious and hostile to Christianity. In addition, he resolved to use Priestley as the instrument for propagating this view of Christianity among the general public in order to foster the social harmony he cherished as one of the bulwarks of the American republic.[63]

Socrates and Jesus galvanized Jefferson into action because it appeared during a period of unusually intense partisan conflict and exceptionally severe attacks on the president's putative infidelity. Spain's retrocession of Louisiana to France and the suspension by Spanish authorities of the American right of deposit at New Orleans had led, during the winter of 1802-1803, to an upsurge of war fever in the normally Republican West, which the Federalists tried to turn to their advantage by sharply criticizing Jefferson for his apparent supineness in the face of a threat to a vital national interest and by loudly calling for the employment of military force to vindicate the country's treaty rights. Although Jefferson allayed Western fears and overcame the immediate crisis by dispatching James Monroe on a special diplomatic mission to France in January 1803, this episode still stood as a stark reminder to him of the dangers that extreme partisanship posed to the often fragile ties that bound together the new nation and once again made him sensitive to the problem of maintaining social harmony in a republican society.[64] Furthermore, while Federalist leaders were calling for war in the West, they and their clerical supporters were also busily denouncing Jefferson as an archenemy of religion with even greater vehemence than usual owing to the return of Thomas Paine to America in October 1802 after a tempestuous absence of fifteen years in Europe. The arrival of the author of the notoriously anti-Christian *Age of Reason* and the warm welcome he received from the president could mean only one thing, the Federalists and their ministerial allies repeated over and over again: Jefferson had brought Paine back to America so that Paine could subvert Christianity in the United States as he supposedly had done in France. A Republican congressman from Virginia vividly described the opposition's onslaught on the president to his constituents several weeks before Jefferson read *Socrates and Jesus:* "The federalist, like a bear with a sore head, or robbed of her whelps, would go all lengths to plunge our happy country into a war, take all occasions to inflame the minds of the people, by doing which they think they can draw the President into contempt; their necromantic art is easily seen through, for though they cry out war, war; and that nothing but war is to secure the port of New-Orleans, in the next breath they say they have no confidence in the President; if war was to be the result, that the President is a coward, a jacobin and infidel; that he is a deist, and all the republican party, or the leaders of them; that the President sent to France for Thomas Paine to destroy religion—this Paine is the author of the Age of Reason." Anxious to reduce the social disharmony caused by partisan and sectarian strife, and provoked beyond endurance by Federalist criticism of his religion, Jefferson welcomed the opportunity provided by *Socrates and Jesus* for revealing his view of Christianity directly to a small number of confidants and indirectly, through Priestley, to the public at large.

Jefferson wasted little time in urging Priestley to write an ironic work on

Christianity that would reflect the president's view of the subject. A few days after reading *Socrates and Jesus*, he dispatched a carefully worded letter to Priestley in which he praised the pamphlet and entreated the author to deal with the same subject "on a more extensive scale." In order to facilitate Priestley's task, he proceeded to outline exactly the sort of work he himself would have liked to write but which, for lack of sufficient time and adequate knowledge, he wanted the Unitarian leader to publish instead. Thus he advised the aged controversialist to begin by examining the moral teachings of the leading Epicurean and Stoic philosophers of antiquity, noting the points in which they excelled as well as those in which they were deficient. This done, the next step was to describe what the president perceived to be the degraded condition of the theology and ethics of the Jews so as to show the need for the reform of both on the eve of Jesus' birth. Only then, he believed, would it be possible to portray Jesus in his true historic role as a great moral reformer who, recognizing the inadequacies of the morality and theology of the Jews, "endeavored to bring them to the principles of a pure deism, and juster notions of the attributes of god, to reform their moral doctrines to the standard of reason, justice and philanthropy, and to inculcate the belief of a future state." Jefferson admonished Priestley to avoid the contentious issue of whether Jesus was a member of the godhead himself or merely a divinely inspired man, well knowing that even he and his Unitarian correspondent did not agree on that point. However, he strongly emphasized the need to point out the difficulties involved in ascertaining the true teachings of Jesus, since, in his view, they were first written down many years after Jesus' death by the "most unlettered of men" and were then further corrupted in the course of time by "those who pretend to be his special disciples." Yet, despite the disrepute into which orthodox Christianity had fallen, at least in Jefferson's opinion, he was confident that a work that accurately described the authentic doctrines of Jesus, restoring them to their original purity and simplicity and eliminating the corruptions of later ages, would convince even the most skeptical that Christian morality was superior to any alternative and that its founder was the "most innocent, the most benevolent the most eloquent and sublime character that ever has been exhibited to man." In addition to serving the cause of historical truth, however, Jefferson obviously hoped that a work such as the one he so painstakingly outlined to Priestley would promote harmonious social relations among the citizens of the young republic by emphasizing the moral imperatives of Jesus that united them rather than the dogmas of the churches that divided them, thereby making religion a centripetal rather than a centrifugal force in the new nation and thus eliminating what the president saw as one of the mainsprings of excessively divisive partisanship in the country.[66]

Less than two weeks after writing to Priestley, Jefferson described his attitude toward Christianity at greater length in a well-known letter to Dr. Rush and an accompanying "Syllabus of an Estimate of the merit of the doctrines of Jesus, compared with those of others."[67] In these two documents, which were written with considerable care, the president offered the first and only formal description of his demythologized Christian faith, which he had developed in part under the influence of Priestley's writings and to which he adhered for the rest of his life. In the letter Jefferson recalled his promise to provide Rush with a statement on his view of Christianity and apologized for taking so long to keep his pledge, citing in extenuation the press of public business as well as the difficulty of the subject. Despite Federalist charges to the contrary, Jefferson denied that he was averse to Christianity and claimed that in fact he was as good a Christian as anyone. But the Christianity he believed in was not the religion professed by the Christian churches. "To the corruptions of Christianity, I am indeed opposed," he confided to his Philadelphia friend, thereby revealing his continued distaste for orthodoxy, "but not to the genuine precepts of Jesus himself. I am a Christian, in the only sense in which he wished any one to be; sincerely attached to his doctrines, in preference to all others; ascribing to himself every human excellence, and believing he never claimed any other." Although he realized this admission might disarm some of those who criticized him on religious grounds, he implored Rush to regard his letter as confidential lest it be construed to mean that he conceded to the public a right to scrutinize his religious beliefs.

Jefferson explained his concept of the "genuine precepts of Jesus" in the "Syllabus" that accompanied his letter to Rush. This document, cast in the form of a comparative analysis of the moral doctrines of the classical philosophers, the Jews, and Jesus, was in effect an elaboration of the views he had expressed in his recent letter to Priestley. Jefferson praised the ancients for their precepts regarding the achievement of self-discipline but found them seriously deficient with respect to man's social obligations. In particular, he criticized their failure to inculcate "peace, charity, and love to our fellow men" or to embrace "with benevolence, the whole family of mankind." Considering his belief in the necessity of maintaining social harmony to ensure the success of America's experiment in self-government, the evaluation was tantamount to admitting that the teachings of the Epicurean and Stoic moralists, which he had once valued above all others, were insufficient for guiding the moral sense of a republican nation. Turning to the Jews, Jefferson gave them due, if somewhat grudging, credit for being monotheists. Otherwise he faulted them for having deplorable ideas of the attributes of God and for adhering to a system of ethics that he judged to be irrational with respect to relations between individuals as well as antisocial in regard to intercourse between nations. As a result, they stood in need of "reformation ... in an eminent degree" at the dawn of the Christian era.

Having thus set the stage, Jefferson next dealt with Jesus. In his view, the Nazarene was the foremost moral reformer of the Jews, and his teachings, he implied, were of universal significance owing to his highly developed moral sense, not his divinity or divine inspiration, neither of which Jefferson accepted. The president reduced the authentic doctrines of Jesus to three essential points. First, this "benevolent and sublime reformer,"[68] as Jefferson was wont to call him, confirmed the monotheism of the Jews while correcting their erroneous notions of the "attributes and government" of the one true God. Next, he preached a system of morality that was far superior to those of the ancients and the Jews in that it dealt with intentions as well as acts and instilled "universal philanthropy, not only to kindred and friends, to neighbors and countrymen, but to all mankind, gathering all into one family, under bonds of love, charity, peace, common wants, and common aids"—a system, in short, that was well designed to promote social concord among a citizenry whose commitment to republican principles and institutions was threatened, in Jefferson's opinion, by partisan and sectarian strife. Finally, he taught the doctrine of a life in the hereafter in order to encourage virtuous conduct in the here and now. Aside from these three points, Jefferson virtually

Syllabus of an Estimate of the merit of the doctrines of Jesus, compared with those of others.

In a comparative view of the Ethics of the enlightened nations of antiquity, of the Jews, and of Jesus, no notice should be taken of the corruptions of reason among the antients, to wit, the idolatry & superstition of their vulgar, Nor of the corruptions of Christianity by the ^{over} learned among it's professors.

Let a just view be taken of the moral principles inculcated by the most esteemed of the sects of ant.^t philosophy, or of their individuals; particularly Pythagoras, Socrates, Epicurus, Cicero, Epictetus, Seneca, Antoninus.

I. Philosophers. 1. Their precepts related chiefly to ourselves, and the government of those passions which, unrestrained, would disturb our tranquility of mind. * in this branch of Philosophy they were really great.

2. In developing our duties to others, they were short and defective. they embraced indeed the circles of kindred & friends: and inculcated patriotism, or the love of our country in the aggregate, as a primary obligation. towards our neighbors & countrymen, they taught justice, but scarcely viewed them as within the circle of benevolence. still less have they inculcated peace, charity, & love to our fellow men, or embraced with benevolence, the whole family of mankind.

II. Jews. 1. Their system was Deism, that is, the belief of one only god. but their ideas of him, & of his attributes, were degrading & injurious.

2. their Ethics were not only imperfect, but often irreconcileable with the sound dictates of reason & morality, as they respect intercourse with those around us. & repulsive, & anti-social, as respecting other nations. they needed reformation therefore in an eminent degree.

III. Jesus. In this state of things among the Jews, Jesus appeared. his parentage was obscure, his condition poor, his education null, his natural endowments great, his life correct & innocent, he was meek, benevolent, patient, firm, disinterested, & of the sublimest eloquence.

The disadvantages under which his doctrines appear are remarkeable.

1. like Socrates & Epictetus, he wrote nothing himself.

2. but he had not, like them, a Xenophon or an Arrian to write for him. on the contrary, all the learned of his country, entrenched in it's power & riches, were opposed to him. lest his labours should undermine their advantages: and the committing to writing his life & doctrines, fell on the most unlettered, & ignorant of men: who wrote too from memory, & not till long after the transactions had passed.

3. according to the ordinary fate of those who attempt to enlighten and reform mankind, he fell an early victim to the jealousy & combination of the altar and the throne: at about 33. years of age, his reason having not yet attained the maximum of it's energy, nor the course of his preaching, which was but of about 3. years, presented occasions for developing a compleat system of morals.

---

* To explain, I will exhibit the heads of Seneca's & Cicero's philosophical works, the most extensive of any we have re-cieved from the antients. of 10. heads in Seneca, 7. relate to ourselves, to wit, de ira, Consolatio, de tranquilitate, de constantia sapientis, de otio sapientis, de vita beata, de brevitate vitae. 2. relate to others, de clementia, de beneficiis. & 1. relates to the govern-ment of the world, de providentia. of 11. tracts of Cicero, 5. respect ourselves, viz. de finibus, Tusculana, Academica, Para-doxa, de Senectute. 1. de officiis, partly to ourselves, partly to others. 1. de amicitia, relates to others: and 4. are on different subjects, to wit, de natura deorum, de divinatione, de fato, Somnium Scipionis.

FIGURE 4. *Thomas Jefferson's "Syllabus for the Merits of the Doctrines of Jesus," page 1 (Thomas Jefferson Papers, Special Collections Department, University of Virginia Library)*

4. Hence the doctrines which he really delivered were defective as a whole.

and fragments only of what he did deliver have come to us, mutilated, mistated, & often unintelligible.

5. they have been still more disfigured by the corruptions of schismatising followers,

who have found an interest in sophisticating & perverting the simple doctrines he taught,

by engrafting on them the mysticisms of a Grecian Sophist, frittering them into subtleties, & obscuring them with jargon,

until they have caused good men to reject the whole in disgust, & to view Jesus himself as an impostor.

Notwithstanding these disadvantages a system of morals is presented to us, which,

if filled up in the true stile and spirit of the rich fragments he left us,

would be the most perfect and sublime that has ever been taught by man.

The question of his being a member of the god-head, or in direct communication with it,

claimed for him by some of his followers, and denied by others,

is foreign to the present view, which is merely an estimate of the intrinsic merit of his doctrines.

1. He corrected the Deism of the Jews, confirming them in their belief of one only god,

and giving them juster notions of his attributes and government.

2. His moral doctrines relating to kindred & friends were more pure & perfect, than those of the most correct of the philosophers,

and greatly more so than those of the Jews.

and they went far beyond both in inculcating universal philanthropy,

not only to kindred and friends, to neighbors and countrymen,

but to all mankind, gathering all into one family, under the bonds of love, charity, peace, common

wants, and common aids. a developement of this head will evince the peculiar superiority

of the system of Jesus over all others.

3. the precepts of Philosophy, & of the Hebrew code, laid hold of actions only.

he pushed his scrutinies into the heart of man; erected his tribunal in the region of his thoughts,

and purified the waters at the fountain head.

4. he taught, emphatically, the doctrine of a future state:

which was either doubted or disbelieved by the Jews.

and wielded it with efficacy, as an important incentive, supplementary to the other motives

to moral conduct.

FIGURE 5. *Thomas Jefferson's "Syllabus for the Merits of the Doctrines of Jesus," page 2 (Thomas Jefferson Papers, Special Collections Department, University of Virginia Library)*

stated that every other doctrine ascribed to Jesus was in reality a corruption of his original message that had resulted either from the unintentional misrepresentations of the Evangelists, who recorded his teachings long after his death, or from the machinations of his "schematizing followers" who deliberately perverted his simple precepts to serve their own ends. Accordingly, the implied message of the "Syllabus" was that Christianity could only be made acceptable to rational men by purging it of its corruptions and restoring the doctrines of Jesus to their pristine simplicity.[69]

Jefferson did not write his letter to Rush and the "Syllabus" simply to keep a promise to a friend. He also used them to convince a few relatives and confidants of the groundlessness of Federalist charges that he was an atheist and an infidel and to test the acceptability of his view of Christianity. At the same time that he dispatched these two documents to Rush, he also sent copies of them to his daughters (Martha Jefferson Randolph and Mary Jefferson Eppes),[70] to at least two members of his cabinet (Secretary of War Henry Dearborn and Attorney General Levi Lincoln) and probably to two more (Secretary of the Treasury Albert Gallatin and Postmaster General Gideon Granger),[71] and to Priestley.[72] Later in the year, moreover, he lent a copy of them to his boyhood friend, John Page, a prominent Episcopalian who was then serving as governor of Virginia.[73] Jefferson notified his daughters and his cabinet members that he wanted them to read the letter and the "Syllabus" so that they could judge for themselves the truth or falsehood of the charges made against him on religious grounds, but he made it clear that he wanted neither document to appear in print. Although Jefferson had no wish to publicize his religious beliefs directly, he was nevertheless eager for Priestley to publish a work on Christianity that would reflect his own views and promote social harmony, and therefore he sent both documents to the Unitarian for the express purpose of encouraging him to undertake this task.[74]

Reaction to the letter to Rush and the "Syllabus," though mixed, was generally encouraging. The response of Jefferson's daughters to them is unknown, but after reading the "Syllabus" Governor Page was pleased to inform Jefferson that he "was not mistaken in my opinion that the difference between us was not so great, as many have supposed."[75] Attorney General Lincoln praised the

"Syllabus" as a "valuable compendium" and received permission from Jefferson to make a copy for his personal use, while Secretary of War Dearborn, mistakenly assuming that the president planned to publish this document to refute his religious critics, advised him to use somewhat more diplomatic language in characterizing the Evangelists.[76] Rush himself expressed pleasure at the discovery that Jefferson was "by no means so heterodox as you have been supposed to be by your enemies," and while rejecting the president's contention that Jesus was merely human, he assured him that he had long since ceased to regard theological exactitude "as the criterion of disposition and Conduct, and much less of our future acceptance at the bar of the supreme Judge of the World."[77] This point of view must have delighted Jefferson, but, as he later learned to his regret, it was not one to which Rush steadily adhered. Jefferson was probably most interested in Priestley's reaction to the letter and the "Syllabus," however, and this, though at first slightly disappointing, was in the end a source of great satisfaction to him. As might have been expected, Priestley vigorously rejected Jefferson's notion that Jesus had never claimed to be acting under a special mission from God, but he treated this as an honest difference of opinion and otherwise found nothing to criticize in Jefferson's view of Christianity. More importantly, although Priestley was initially reluctant to accept Jefferson's "flattering invitation to enter farther into the comparison of Jesus with other philosophers," he subsequently changed his mind and informed the president in December 1803 that he had decided to write such a comparative study after all.[78]

Jefferson was sufficiently encouraged by the response to the limited disclosure of his demythologized Christian faith to turn to the task of extracting the passages from the Gospels that he regarded as expressive of the authentic teachings of Jesus. Having decided that a rationalized variant of Christianity purged of what he saw as its corruptions was not only preferable to any other religion but also potentially one of the strongest unifying forces in a republican society, the naturally methodical Jefferson felt impelled to determine with exact precision the genuine moral precepts of Jesus, which for him constituted the heart of the Christian religion, and thereby rid them of the unpalatable mystifications with which Jesus' followers had allegedly surrounded them throughout history. Jefferson approached this task with his usual care and preparation. As early as 9 April 1803, the same day he had first urged Priestley to write a work on Christianity, he ordered from a Philadelphia bookseller two volumes by the Unitarian theologian that were well designed to facilitate his study of the Gospels—*A Harmony of the Evangelists in English* and *A Harmony of the Evangelists in Greek*. Then, after being informed that these works were not readily available, he renewed his request for them on 5 May, just as he was receiving the first reactions to the letter to Rush and the "Syllabus."[79] He finally obtained the *Harmonies* from Priestley himself, who, learning of Jefferson's failure to obtain them, sent him a personal copy of the two works in August, though it is uncertain exactly when they arrived.[80] For the remainder of the year Jefferson was too preoccupied with public business to pursue his biblical researches, and it seems that he did not begin this work in earnest until after he learned in December that Priestley had embarked on a study of classical and Christian morality. With the assistance of Priestley's *Harmonies*, Jefferson then started to examine the Gospels, distinguishing what he considered to be the true from the false teachings of Jesus, until at length, by 20 January 1804, he decided he was ready to make a compilation in Greek and English of the biblical passages containing Jesus' genuine moral precepts. On that day he ordered "two copies of the New Testament in Greek or Greek and Latin, both of the same edition exactly; and two others in English, both also of the same edition and all four of the same format that they may admit of being bound up together."[81]

As Jefferson awaited the arrival of the New Testaments he had ordered, he hastened to apprise Priestley of what now appeared to him to be a serious omission in the concept of the work on Christianity that he had earlier outlined for the use of his Unitarian friend. In consequence of his study of the Gospels, Jefferson was now convinced that Priestley's work could best serve the twin causes of religious truth and social harmony if it contained an introductory section consisting of the moral teachings of Jesus expressed in the *ipsima verba* of the great reformer himself. "I rejoice that you have undertaken the task of comparing the moral doctrines of Jesus with those of the ancient Philosophers," he wrote to Priestley near the end of January, adding: "I think you cannot avoid giving, as preliminary to the comparison, a digest of his moral doctrines, extracted in his own words from the Evangelists, and leaving out everything relative to his personal history and character. It would be short and precious."[82] Jefferson even intimated that he was willing to put aside his own plan to make a compilation of extracts from the Gospels if Priestley followed his suggestion. Priestley died on 6 February, however, before receiving the president's letter but after completing his comparative study of ancient and Christian morality, whereupon Jefferson decided to go ahead with his original plan.[83]

Jefferson completed his first collection of Gospel extracts—"The Philosophy of Jesus"—with remarkable dispatch. On 4 February 1804 he received two sets of the New Testament—a pair of virtually identical English editions published in Dublin by George Grierson in 1791 and 1799 as well as two copies of a Greek-Latin edition published in London by F. Wingrave and others in 1794— and by 10 March the compilation was finished and bound.[84] Little is known about the actual composition of this work. Jefferson apparently first made a list of the Gospel verses that seemed to him to contain the genuine moral teachings of Jesus, and then, over a period of several evenings, he clipped these passages from the Bible and added others as he went along, pasting them in double columns on 46 octavo sheets.[85] Contrary to his original design, he only used verses in English, evidently deciding that the press of public business left him with insufficient time to produce a bilingual text. Although many distinguished biblical scholars have been daunted by the challenge of disentangling the many layers of the New Testament, the rationalistic Jefferson was supremely confident of his ability to differentiate between the true and the false precepts of Jesus, observing on several occasions that the former were "as easily distinguishable as diamonds in a dunghill."[86] His first biblical compilation, he was convinced, contained nothing but "46. pages of pure and unsophisticated doctrines, such as were professed and acted on by the unlettered apostles, the Apostolic fathers, and the Christians of the 1st century."[87] He entitled it "The Philosophy of Jesus of Nazareth extracted from the account of his life and doctrines as given by Matthew, Mark, Luke, and John. being an abridgment of the New Testament for the use of the Indians unembarrassed with matters of fact or faith beyond the level of their comprehensions." This subtitle was intentionally ironic. The "Indians" Jefferson had in mind were

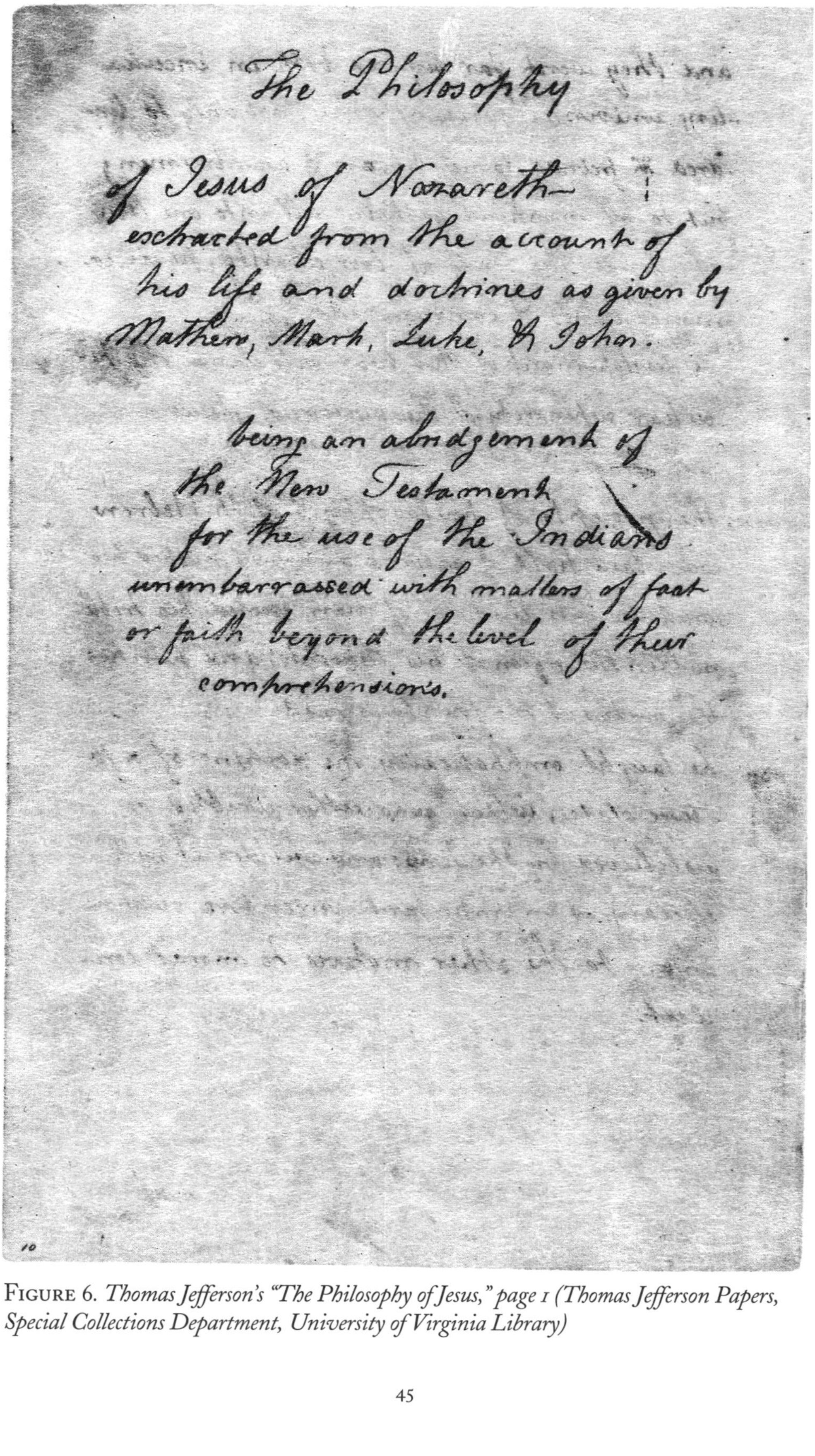

The Philosophy

of Jesus of Nazareth
extracted from the account of
his life and doctrines as given by
Matthew, Mark, Luke, & John.

being an abridgement of
the New Testament
for the use of the Indians
unembarrassed with matters of fact
or faith beyond the level of their
comprehension.

10

FIGURE 6. *Thomas Jefferson's "The Philosophy of Jesus," page 1 (Thomas Jefferson Papers, Special Collections Department, University of Virginia Library)*

A Table of the texts extracted from the gospels, of the order in which they are arranged into sections, & the heads of each section.

§. I. Luke 2. 1—7. 21. 22. 39—49. 51. 52 } History of Jesus.
         3. 23—38.

II. Matt. 10. 5—31. 42. Precepts for the Priesthood.

III. Luke 22. 24—27. } Preachers to be humble.
      John. 13. 4—17. }

IV. John. 10. 1—16 }
     Luke. 11. 52. } false teachers.
          12. 13—15 }

V. John. 13. 34. 35. disciples should love one another.

VI. Matt. 13. 24—30. 36—43. Parable of the tares.
    man not to judge for God.

VII. Matt. 20. 1—16. Parable of the laborers.

VIII. Mark. 2. 15—17. } Physicians are for the sick.
      Matt. 18. 10. 11 } Parables of the lost sheep, the
      Luke 15. 3—32. } lost peice of silver the proodigal son.

IX. John. 8. 1—11. }
     matt. 18. 15—17. } the duty of mutual forgiveness
     Luke. 13. 6—9 } & forbearance.

X. matt. 5. 1—10. 19—48. }
        6. 1—34 } the Sermon in the mount;
        7. 1—27.

FIGURE 7. *Thomas Jefferson's "The Philosophy of Jesus," page 2 (Thomas Jefferson Papers, Special Collections Department, University of Virginia Library)*

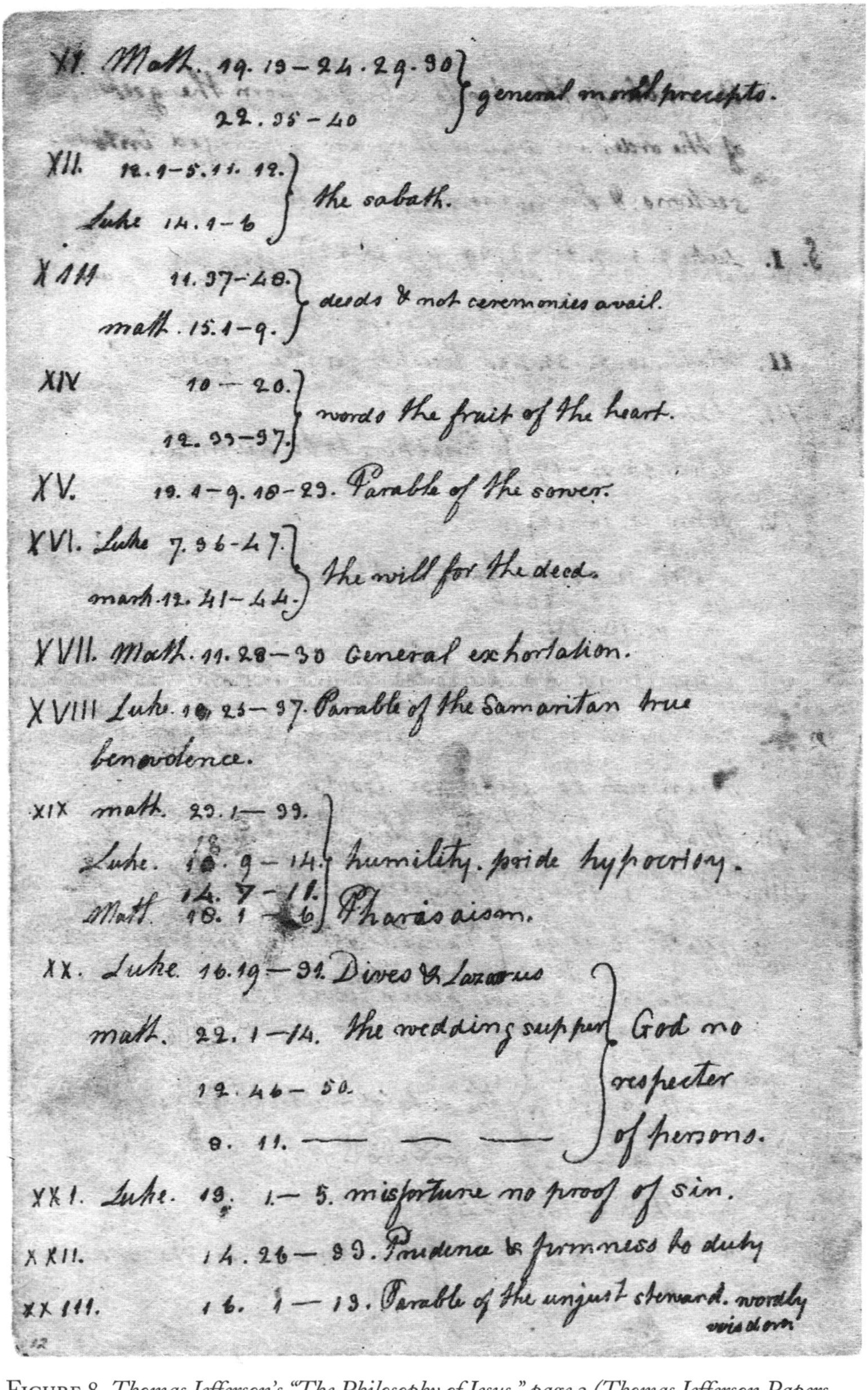

XI. Matt. 19. 13 — 24. 29. 30 } general moral precepts.
22. 35 — 40

XII. 12. 1 — 5. 11. 12. } the sabath.
Luke 14. 1 — 6

XIII. 11. 37 — 48. } deeds & not ceremonies avail.
matt. 15. 1 — 9.

XIV. 10 — 20. } words the fruit of the heart.
12. 33 — 37.

XV. 13. 1 — 9. 18 — 23. Parable of the sower.

XVI. Luke 7. 36 — 47. } the will for the deed.
mark. 12. 41 — 44.

XVII. Matt. 11. 28 — 30 General exhortation.

XVIII Luke. 10. 25 — 37. Parable of the Samaritan true
benevolence.

XIX math. 23. 1 — 33. }
Luke. 18. 9 — 14. } humility. pride hypocrisy.
Matt. 18. 1 — 6. } Pharisaism.

XX. Luke. 16. 19 — 31. Dives & Lazarus

matt. 22. 1 — 14. the wedding supper } God no
19. 46 — 50. } respecter
9. 11. —— —— —— } of persons.

XXI. Luke. 13. 1 — 5. misfortune no proof of sin.

XXII. 14. 26 — 33. Prudence & firmness to duty

XXIII. 16. 1 — 13. Parable of the unjust steward. worldly
wisdom

FIGURE 8. *Thomas Jefferson's "The Philosophy of Jesus," page 3 (Thomas Jefferson Papers,
Special Collections Department, University of Virginia Library)*

XXIV.   18.   1—8 . Parable of the unjust judge.

XXV. Matt. 21. 33.—41. Parable of the unjust husbandman & their lord.

XXVI. Luke. 17.   7 — 10. mere justice no praise.

XXVII   14. 12 — 14. The merit of disinterested good.

XXVIII matt. 21. 28 — 31. acts better than proffessions.

XXIX.   22. 15.— 22. submission to magistrates.

XXX: 19. 3 — 12. the bond of mariage.

XXXI.   25. 14 — 30. the duty of improving our talents.

XXXII. Luke. 12. 16 — 21. vain calculations of life.

XXXIII Matt. 24. 1 — 13. ⎫
                                              ⎬ watch and be ready.
        Luke. 12   35 — 48. ⎭

XXXIIII John. 12. 24 — 23. a future life.

XXXV matt   22. 28 — 32. the resurrection.

XXXVI.   25. 31 — 46.   the last judgement.

XXXVII.   18.   31 — 33. 44. 2. the Kingdom of heaven

XXXVIII John. 4.   24. God.

XXXIX. John 18. 1.2.3. Matt. 26. 49. 50 John 18. 4. 5. 8.

        Matt. 26. 55. John. 18. 12. Matt. 26. 57.

        John. 18. 19 — 23. matt. 26. 59 — 62. Luke. 22. 67. 68. 70.

        mark. 14. 60. 64. Luke. 23. 1 — 3. John 18. 36.

        Luke 23. 4 — 23. Matt 27. 24. 25. Luke 23. 23. 24.

        Matt 27. 26.   John 19. 16.   Luke 23. 33. 34.

        John 19. 25 — 27. matt 27. 46. John 19. 28 — 30.   } death of Jesus.

FIGURE 9. *Thomas Jefferson's "The Philosophy of Jesus," page 4 (Thomas Jefferson Papers, Special Collections Department, University of Virginia Library)*

not the aboriginal inhabitants of North America. They were, rather, the Federalists and their clerical allies, whose political and religious obscurantism, as the president saw it, endangered the stability of the republic and needed to be reformed by a return to the simple, uncorrupted morality of Jesus.[88]

After finishing "The Philosophy of Jesus," Jefferson looked forward with anticipation to the appearance of Priestley's last work on Christianity. But when several months passed and the promised work still had not materialized, Jefferson felt impelled once again to test the acceptability of his nationalistic version of the Christian message. Accordingly, he wrote to Rush early in August 1804 and offered to let him read "The Philosophy of Jesus."[89] Jefferson may have hoped that if Rush approved of this compilation he could be induced to publish a work embodying its view of Christianity. If this was indeed Jefferson's hope, Rush's reply must have come as a rude jolt. For, eschewing the spirit of doctrinal tolerance with which he had greeted the "Syllabus," Rush sternly informed the president that although he would "receive with pleasure the publication you have promised me upon the character of the Messiah ... unless it advances it to divinity and renders his death as well as his life necessary for the restoration of mankind, I shall not accord with its author."[90] Since there was no way "The Philosophy of Jesus" could meet such an exacting standard, Jefferson decided not to send it to his Philadelphia friend after all and never again mentioned the subject in his correspondence with him.

Rush's lack of sympathy for Jefferson's demystified Christian creed was followed by an even more shattering blow to the president's hope of using Christian morality to foster social concord in the new nation. Near the end of 1804 Priestley's comparative analysis of classical and Christian morality was finally published under the title *The Doctrines of Heathen Philosophy, Compared with Those of Revelation.* This work, upon which Jefferson had placed so much hope, disappointed him greatly. It was long, diffuse, and badly written, reflecting the fact that Priestley had composed it while in poor health and facing the shadow of death. It was bogged down by lengthy discussion of often abstruse philosophical and theological points. It made no comparison between Judaism and Christianity, as Jefferson had suggested, and, worst of all from his point of view, it lacked a clear and compact description of the authentic teachings of Jesus. In short, it was useless as a means of promoting the rationalistic Christian faith Jefferson favored. "I apprehend however," he regretfully observed shortly after reading *The Doctrines of Heathen Philosophy*, "that [Priestley] meditated a 2d. part which should have given a view of the genuine doctrines of Jesus divested of those engrafted into his by false followers. I suppose this because it is wanting to compleat the work, and because I observe he calls what is published Part Ist."[91]

Rush's unsympathetic reaction to rationalistic Christianity and Jefferson's disappointment with Priestley's posthumously published work led him to abandon his rather naive hope of promoting social harmony in the young republic by exalting Christian morality over Christian dogma. Rush's response suggested the futility of trying to propagate a version of Christianity that sought to evade the central issue of Jesus' divinity, and Priestley's death deprived the president of the only trusted friend with theological ability who was sympathetic to his religious views. Jefferson himself continued to be averse to religious controversy and thus had no intention of personally publicizing his view of Christianity beyond the limited circle to which he had already revealed it. At the same time, Jefferson's overwhelming victory in the presidential election of 1804, coupled with the continued growth of the Republican party throughout the nation, temporarily allayed his apprehensions about the future of republicanism in the United States, while the various domestic and international crises that punctuated his second administration diverted him from further intensive study of the New Testament. Thus, although he remained deeply interested in ascertaining the authentic moral teachings of Jesus, henceforth he pursued this subject for personal rather than public reasons. After 1804, except in a single instance discussed below, he used "The Philosophy of Jesus" strictly for his private moral instruction and edification, until at length he replaced it with a more ambitious compilation, "The Life and Morals of Jesus."

III

Aside from the fact that both were part of Jefferson's quest for the genuine doctrines of Jesus, in virtually every other important respect "The Philosophy of Jesus" and "The Life and Morals of Jesus" stand in sharp contrast to each other. The main focus of "The Philosophy of Jesus" is on the moral teachings of Jesus, whereas "The Life and Morals of Jesus" gives attention to the details of his career as well as the content of his doctrine. Jefferson compiled "The Philosophy of Jesus" in response to his personal religious needs and his concern with the problem of maintaining social harmony in a republican nation, but "The Life and Morals of Jesus" was strictly a product of his private search for religious truth. "The Philosophy of Jesus" is a unilingual compilation of Gospel verses in English, whereas "The Life and Morals of Jesus" is a multilingual collection of verses in Greek, Latin, French, and English (Jefferson did not read Hebrew or any other Semitic language). The provenance of "The Philosophy of Jesus" is fairly clear, and the date of its compilation can be determined with great exactitude; the background of "The Life and Morals of Jesus" is more obscure, and the precise date of its composition still cannot be established with any certainty. The steps that led Jefferson to compile "The Life and Morals of Jesus" continue to be somewhat unclear, but they include his correspondence with John Adams, an exchange of letters with the former secretary of the Continental Congress, the importunities of an immigrant Dutch scholar, Jefferson's interest in the progress of Unitarianism, and a chance remark by a man he had once cherished like a son.

Jefferson seems to have initially conceived the idea of making a quadrilingual compilation of Gospel verses shortly before he began his second term as president. In order to accomplish such a work he first had to acquire two copies of the New Testament in each of the languages he planned to use. This was of paramount importance because in the process of clipping verses from the Evangelists and pasting them onto blank sheets of paper it was inevitable that he would occasionally take some passages from one side of a given page and then later decide to use others on the reverse side of it, thus forcing him to have recourse to a second, unclipped copy of the same page. Accordingly, he instructed a Baltimore book-seller at the end of January 1805 to send him two copies of "le Nouveau testament corrigé sur le Grec in 12mo. Paris. 1803," carefully noting that "a single one, or two of different editions would not answer to my purpose,"[92] and a few weeks later he ordered the same number of copies of "a tolerably decent edition of the New testament in 12mo." from a Philadelphia book dealer.[93] Since these orders were promptly filled, Jefferson had in his possession by the end of March dual copies of a French New Testament printed in Paris in 1802 by J. Smith and of an English New Testament printed in Philadelphia in 1804 by Jacob Johnson.[94] These, together with the pair of identical Greek-Latin New Testaments he had acquired the year before in connection with "The Philosophy of Jesus," gave him the basic sources he needed to make a quadrilingual biblical compilation and were in fact the very same volumes he used to compile "The Life and Morals of Jesus" during his retirement at Monticello a decade and a half later.[95] Unfortunately, Jefferson never explained why, after having taken the trouble early in 1805 to gather the materials for a more linguistically comprehensive collection of extracts from the Gospels than that contained in "The Philosophy of Jesus," he put aside the projected work and did not take it up again in earnest for another fifteen years. He was probably too busy attending to affairs of state during his second adminis-tration as president to find time for further biblical research, and he apparently found "The Philosophy of Jesus" sufficiently satisfying as a source of moral in-struction during the early years of his retirement from public life to obviate the need for another work of this sort.[96] In the absence of direct evidence, however, any account for this delay must be necessarily conjectural.

After he retired from the presidency, Jefferson's revived correspondence with John Adams was the next step in the path that eventually led to "The Life and Morals of Jesus." After a hiatus of eleven years caused by their political estrange-ment during the 1790s, the two ex-presidents resumed writing to each other in 1812, largely through the devoted efforts of their mutual friend, Benjamin Rush.[97] The subject of Christianity soon became one of the leading themes of their corre-spondence as a result of the printing of Jefferson's 9 April 1803 letter to Joseph

Priestley in Thomas Belsham's *Memoirs of the Late Reverend Theophilus Lindsey*, a biography of one of the founding fathers of English Unitarianism that was published in London in 1812.[98] Adams, who had also rejected Christian orthodoxy as a young man,[99] read this letter in the following year and was favorably impressed by Jefferson's estimate of the merits of Christianity in relation to ancient philosophy and Judaism. Adams was unaware of the "Syllabus" or the posthumous publication of Priestley's *The Doctrines of Heathen Philosophy, Compared with Those of Revelation*, however, and he expressed regret that Jefferson had never elaborated his view of Christianity to Rush and that Priestley had failed to publish the comparative analysis of classical, Jewish, and Christian morality that Jefferson had urged him to write. Jefferson thereupon sought to dispel these misapprehensions by sending Adams a copy of the "Syllabus" and *The Doctrines of Heathen Philosophy* as well as by giving him the first detailed description of "The Philosophy of Jesus." Like Jefferson, Adams was disappointed by Priestley's last book, but he admired the "Syllabus" and urged Jefferson several times to publish a comparative study of classical and Christian morality that would set forth this view of the authentic teachings of Jesus. But Jefferson deftly turned aside Adams' pleas, citing old age and insufficient knowledge of the subject in justification of his refusal to undertake this task, to which he also might have added his settled resolve never to reveal his religious beliefs to the public. "We must leave therefore to others, younger and more learned than we are," he informed Adams in the fall of 1813, "to prepare this euthanasia for Platonic Christianity, and it's restoration to the primitive simplicity of it's founder."[100] Despite Jefferson's refusal to write a book on religion in accordance with Adams' wishes, this episode led to a wide-ranging discussion of fundamental religious issues by the two elder statesmen that lasted almost until the time of their deaths. Both agreed that Christianity was originally a simple system of moral teachings that had to be purged of the dogmatic corruptions of later ages in order to be made intellectually respectable to rational men, thereby encouraging Jefferson to persist in his quest for the genuine doctrines of Jesus.[101]

Adams' repeated calls for Jefferson to publish a comparison of the moral doctrines of antiquity and Christianity did not fall upon entirely deaf ears. To be sure, Jefferson never planned to write a book on this subject for publication, but he did reexamine "The Philosophy of Jesus" and tentatively decide to revise it in a manner that somewhat reflected Adams' influence, having concluded by 1816 that it "was too hastily done ... being the work of one or two evenings only, while I lived at Washington, overwhelmed with other business."[102] Jefferson first revealed this decision to his old friend Charles Thomson, who had served as secretary to the Continental Congress from its inception in 1774 to its demise in 1789 and then retired from politics to devote the rest of his life to biblical scholarship. He produced a highly regarded translation of the Bible that was published in 1808 and a *Synopsis of the Four Evangelists* that appeared seven years later.[103] Shortly after receiving a copy of the latter from his former colleague in the Old Congress, Jefferson thanked Thomson for the gift in a letter written early in January 1816, in which he briefly described "The Philosophy of Jesus," adducing it as "a document in proof that I am a *real Christian*, that is to say, a disciple of the doctrines of Jesus, very different from the Platonists, who call *me* infidel, and *themselves* Christians and preachers of the gospel, while they draw all their characteristic dogmas from what it's Author never said or saw." He then noted that if he could find the time he wanted to add to "The Philosophy of Jesus" the corresponding Greek, Latin, and French verses "in columns side by side," which would have entailed redoing the whole work since there was probably not enough room in the original compilation for three more columns of Gospel verses. He also wanted to subjoin to the revised compilation a translation of Pierre Gassendi's *Syntagma Epicuri Philosphiae*, a seventeenth-century volume by a French Catholic priest and philosopher that contained a Christianized version of Epicureanism that Jefferson greatly admired inasmuch as he regarded the teachings of Epicurus as "the most rational system remaining of the philosophy of the ancients, as frugal of vicious indulgence, and fruitful of virtue as the hyperbolic extravagancies of his rival sects."[104] If Jefferson had in fact altered "The Philosophy of Jesus" along these lines, the resulting work would have borne some resemblance to the comparative study of classical and Christian morality that Adams had urged him to produce, with the important exception that it would have been strictly for Jefferson's personal use. Jefferson informed another correspondent several months later that he definitely planned to revise "The Philosophy of Jesus" during the winter of 1816-17, but he failed to carry out this resolve for another three years, at which time he produced a much different biblical compilation.[105]

Jefferson's letter to Thomson unexpectedly turned out to be a source of unwelcome publicity for the former president. Thomson, who was old and not in complete possession of his mental faculties, led some of his friends in Pennsylvania to believe that Jefferson had embraced orthodox Christianity, and he inadvertently left the letter itself in the home of a friend in Philadelphia, who apparently allowed others to read it. Rumors thereupon began to circulate that Jefferson had accepted the divinity of Jesus and planned to publish a book on his moral teachings, in consequence of which he received a number of letters inquiring as to the veracity of these reports.[106] Jefferson was distressed by the disclosure of his letter to Thomson, though he generously refrained from criticizing his aged and infirm friend. On the other hand, he indignantly denied any suggestion that the letter signified an alteration in his religious views. "A change from what?" he asked one long-time friend who had written to him in the summer of 1816 regarding his reported conversion to Christian orthodoxy. "The priests indeed have heretofore thought proper to ascribe to me religious, or rather antireligious sentiments, of their own fabric, but such as soothed their resentments against the Act of Virginia for establishing religious freedom .... But I have ever thought religion a concern purely between our god and our consciences, for which we were accountable to him, and not to the priests."[107] He also rejected with equal vehemence the notion that he had written a book on Jesus' doctrines for public consumption. "I write nothing for publication, and last of all things should it be on the subject of religion," he wrote in the fall of the same year to a Philadelphian who had offered to print the work the ex-president had supposedly prepared for publication. "On the dogmas of religion as distinguished from moral principles, all mankind, from the beginning of the world to this day, have been quarrelling, fighting, burning and torturing one another, for abstractions unintelligible to themselves and to all others, and absolutely beyond the comprehension of the human mind. Were I to enter on that arena, I should only add an unit to the number of Bedlamites."[108] Jefferson's stern denials eventually laid to rest the rumors excited by his letter to Thomson, and after 1816 he was no longer troubled by queries about his alleged conversion to traditional Trinitarian Christianity. Nevertheless, this episode probably brought him closer to making a new collection of extracts from the evangelists by strengthening his resolve to produce a private work that embodied his demythologized view of the figure he regarded as the greatest moral teacher in human history rather than the more orthodox view that certain Christians had inferred from the letter to Thomson.

Jefferson was further impelled to compile "The Life and Morals of Jesus" by the failure of his efforts to induce another author to write a rationalistic biography of the founder Christianity. The author in question was Francis Adrian Van der Kemp, a learned Dutch scholar, a former minister with a Unitarian theological outlook, a member of the American Philosophical Society and the American Academy of Arts and Sciences, and an enthusiastic supporter of American independence who had left his homeland to escape political oppression and settled in upstate New York in 1788.[109] The sexagenarian Van der Kemp was a good friend of John Adams and a sometime correspondent of Jefferson who had a penchant for conceiving grandiose works in history, theology, and natural philosophy and then failing to bring them to fruition—a personal foible of which Jefferson was as yet unaware. Van der Kemp did complete one manuscript life of Jesus, but it was never printed because the sole copy was lost in transit when he sent it to England for publication. Subsequently, in 1813, Adams allowed Van der Kemp to read the "Syllabus," disregarding a strict injunction from Jefferson to show it to no one else but Mrs. Adams, though Adams did refuse Van der Kemp's request for a copy of it.[110] This manuscript reawakened Van der Kemp's interest in writing another work on the same subject, and three years later, after having read Jefferson's 9 April 1803 letter to Priestley in Belsham's biography of Theophilus Lindsey, he decided to take direct action. Accordingly, he wrote to Jefferson in March 1816 and not only asked for a copy of the "Syllabus" to use in connection with a life of Jesus he planned to write, but also requested permission to publish the document, without attribution, in a Unitarian journal in England to promote a discussion of Jesus' true merits.[111]

Van der Kemp's announced intention to write a life of Jesus came as welcome news to Jefferson. The former president was still disinclined to publicize his own demystified view of the Nazarene, but he was eager for someone else to publish a book portraying Jesus as a great moral reformer rather than as the son of God, hoping thereby to advance the cause of rational religion and begin the process of ridding Christianity of what he deemed to be its corruptions. Unaware of the frequent disparity between Van der Kemp's scholarly goals and achievements, he somewhat naively concluded that the Unitarian scholar was well suited for this task and therefore went to great lengths to ensure that the projected study of Jesus conformed to his own view of the matter. Thus he gave Van der Kemp permission to publish in England the "Syllabus" and the accompanying 21 April 1803 letter to Benjamin Rush, subject to the stipulation that the authorship of both documents be concealed. He also offered to allow Van der Kemp to print both the "Syllabus" and "The Philosophy of Jesus" in his planned study of Jesus, again on condition that their author remain anonymous. "To this Syllabus and Extract ['The Philosophy of Jesus'], if a history of his life can be added, written with the same view of the subject," he assured this prospective biographer of Jesus, "the world will see, after the fogs shall be dispelled, in which for 14. centuries he has been inveloped by Jeglers to make money of him, when the genuine character shall be exhibited, which they have dressed up in the rags of an Impostor, the world, I say, will at length see the immortal merit of this first of human Sages."[112] Moreover, when Van der Kemp subsequently expressed doubt that he could write an adequate study of Jesus without dealing with a number of related historical and theological issues that he felt ill-equipped to handle, Jefferson sought to dispel his misgivings by urging him to focus his attention on the "mortal biography of Jesus," arguing that such a work, if "candidly and rationally written, without any regard to sectarian dogmas, would reconcile to his character a weighty multitude who do not properly estimate it; and would lay the foundation of a genuine christianity."[113]

Despite all of Jefferson's efforts, Van der Kemp bitterly disappointed his expectations. He did arrange for the publication of the "Syllabus" and the letter to Rush, both suitably altered to conceal the identity of their author, in the October 1816 issue of the *Monthly Repository of Theology and General Literature*, an English

Unitarian periodical. Contrary to Jefferson's hopes, however, they failed to elicit any comment in England, and, evidently owing to an indiscretion by Van der Kemp, they were published with a prefatory statement by the editor of the periodical describing their author as "an eminent American Statesman" who was one of the "leading men in the American revolution."[114] This clue enabled John Quincy Adams, then serving as American ambassador to the Court of St. James, to identify Jefferson as the author of these documents and caused Jefferson to fear that his secret would become known to others—a fate he was spared thanks to the limited circulation of the *Monthly Repository*.[115] Furthermore, Van der Kemp failed to avail himself of Jefferson's invitation to use "The Philosophy of Jesus"—the second and last time that Jefferson offered to allow someone else to read this compilation—and never wrote his projected life of Jesus, adding yet another item to a long list of unexecuted scholarly plans. By the end of 1817, if not before, Jefferson realized that Van der Kemp was not going to produce a study of Jesus and that he himself was the only one who could compile the "mortal biography" of the great reformer to his own satisfaction.[116]

Jefferson's view of the significance of the American Unitarian movement further persuaded him of the value of such a work. He carefully followed the controversy between Calvinists and Unitarians in New England, which became particularly acute after 1815, and rejoiced in any progress the latter made at the expense of the former. He welcomed the Unitarian rejection of the Trinity and its emphasis on the moral precepts of Jesus over the dogmas of the churches, seeing in this the harbinger of a return to the pristine purity of primitive Christianity—a prospect in which he took great pleasure. "The religion of Jesus is founded on the Unity of God, and this principle chiefly, gave it triumph over the rabble of heathen gods then acknoleged," he informed the Rev. Jared Sparks, a Unitarian minister. "Thinking men of all nations rallied readily to the doctrine of one only god, and embraced it with the pure morals which Jesus inculcated."[117] Jefferson was convinced that a similar process was at work in early nineteenth-century America, and therefore he predicted a much more glorious future for Unitarianism than it was in fact to enjoy. "The pure and simple unity of the creator of the universe is now all but ascendant in the Eastern states," he prophesied in 1822, "it is dawning

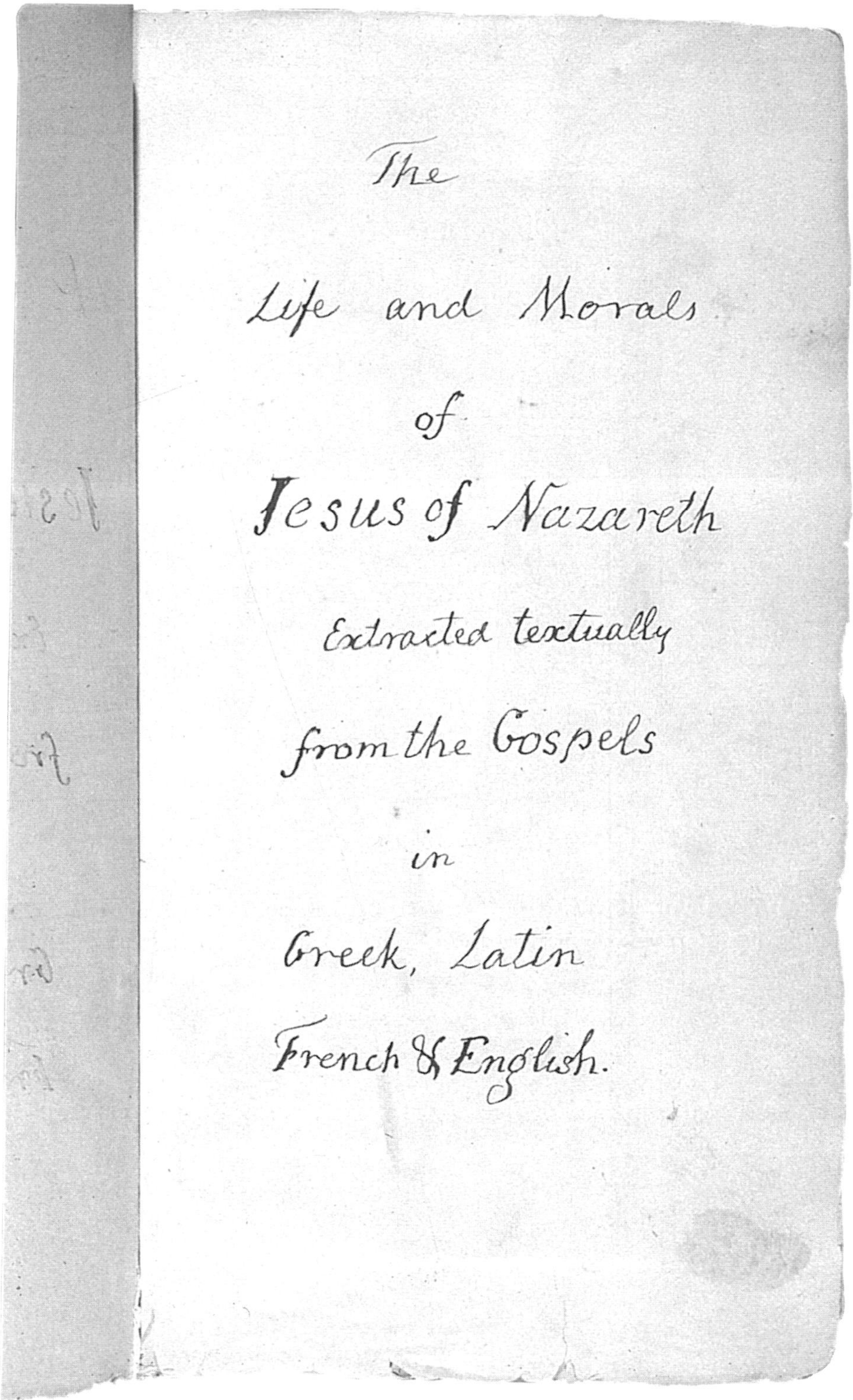

The

Life and Morals

of

Jesus of Nazareth

Extracted textually

from the Gospels

in

Greek, Latin

French & English.

FIGURE 10. *Title Page, Thomas Jefferson's "The Life and Morals of Jesus" (Smithsonian Institution)*

A Table
of the Texts of this ~~Extract~~ from the Evangelists, and of the order of their arrangement.

page	
1.	Luke. 2. 1 — 7. Joseph & Mary go to Bethlehem, where Jesus is born
	21. 39. he is circumcised & named & they return to Nazareth
	40. 42 — 48. 51. 52. at 12 years of age he accompanies his
2.	parents to Jerusalem and returns.
	L. 3. 1. 2. Mk. 1. 6. M. 3. 4. 5. 6. John baptises in Jordan.
	M. 3. 13. Jesus is baptised. L. 3. 23. at 30. years of age.
3.	J. 2. 12 — 16. drives the traders out of the temple.
	J. 3. 22. M. 4. 12. Mk. 6. 17 — 28. he baptises but retires into Galilee on the death of Jn.
4.	~~~~ Mk. 1. 21. 22. he teaches in the Synagogue.
5.	M. 12. 1 — 5. 9 — 12. Mk. 2. 27. M. 12. 14. 15. explains the Sabbath.
	L. 6. 12 — 17. call of his disciples.
6. to 15.	M. 5. 1 — 12. L. 6. 24. 25. 26. M. 5. 13 — 47. L. 6. 34. 35. 36. M. 6. 1 — 34. 7. 1. L. 6. 38. M. 7 3 — 20. 12. 35. 36. 37 7. 24 — 29. the Sermon in the Mount M. 8. 1. Mk. 6. 6. M. 11. 28. 29. 30. exhorts.
16.	L. 7. 36 — 46. a woman anointeth him.
17.	Mk. 3. 31 — 35. L. 12. 1 — 7. 13 — 15 precepts
18.	L. 12. 16 — 21. parable of the rich man.
20	L. 13. 1 — 5 22 — 48. 54. 59. precepts.
21.	L. 13. 6 — 9. parable of the fig tree.
22.	L. 11. 37 — 46. 52. 53. 54. precepts.
23.	M. 13. 1 — 9. Mk. 4. 10. M. 13. 18 — 23. parable of the Sower.
25	Mk. 4. 21. 22. 23. precepts. M. 13. 24 — 30. 36 — 52. parable of the Tares
27	Mk. 4. 26 — 34. L. 9. 57 — 62. L. 5. 27 — 29. Mk. 2. 15 — 17 precepts
	L. 5. 36 — 39. parable of new wine in old bottles.
28	M. 13. 53 — 57 a prophet hath no honor in his own country.
29	M. 9. 36 Mk. 6. 7 M. 10. 5. 6. 9 — 18. 23. 26 — 31. Mk. 6. 12. 30. mission, instrn, return, &ca
30. 31.	J. 7. 1. Mk. 7. 1 — 5. 14 — 24. M. 18. 1 — 4. 7 — 9. 12 — 17. 21 — 22. 5 precepts.
33.	M. 18. 23. — 35. parable of the wicked servant.

FIGURE II. *Table of Contents, Thomas Jefferson's "The Life and Morals of Jesus" (Smithsonian Institution)*

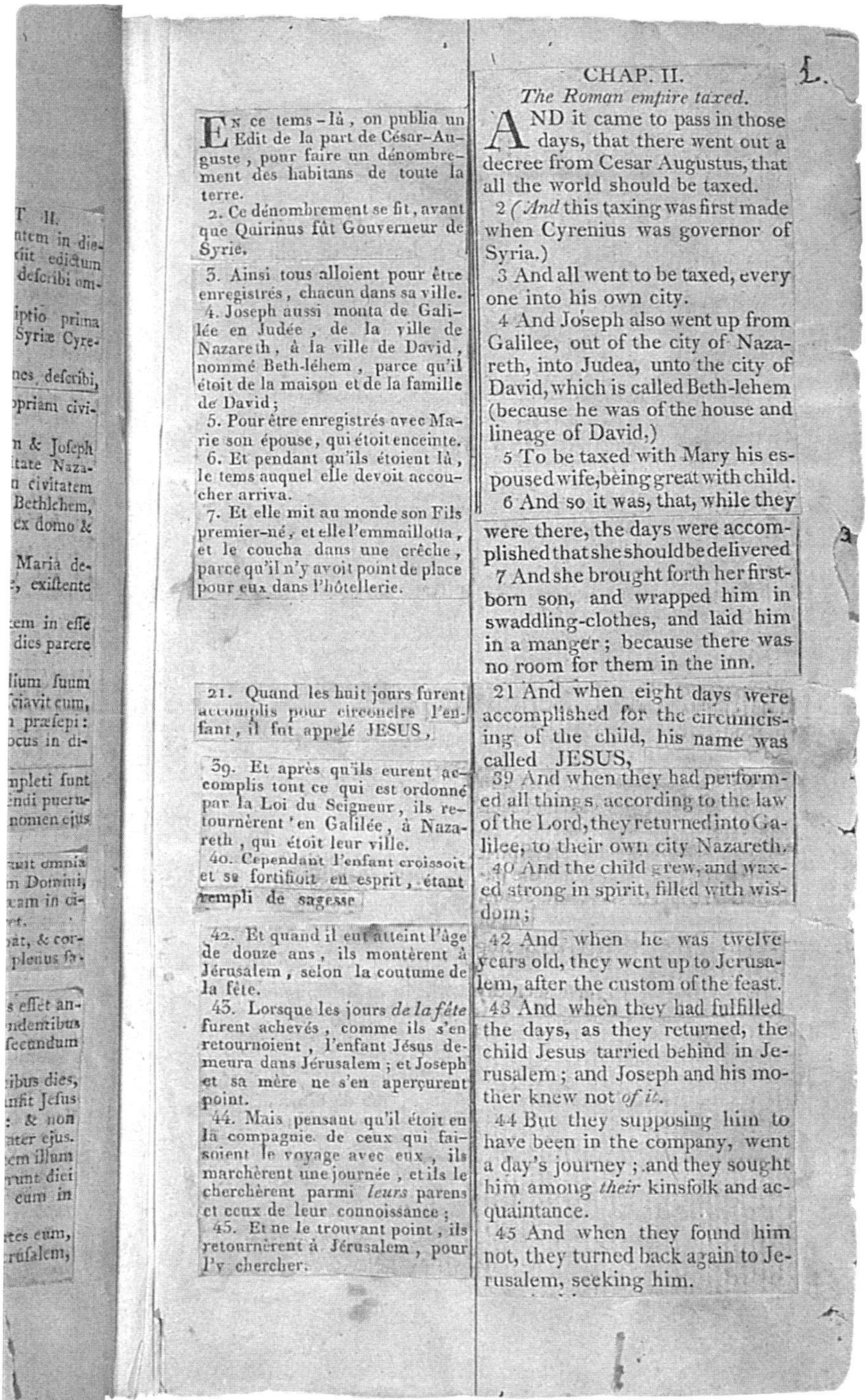

The Roman empire taxed.

Latin (left column, partially visible):

T II.
atem in die
rit edictum
deferibi om-

iptio prima
Syriæ Cyre-

nes deferibi,

opriam civi-

n & Joseph
tate Naza-
a civitatem
Bethlehem,
ex domo &

Maria de-
, exiftente

em in effe
dies parere

lium fuum
ciavit eum,
a præfepi:
ocus in di-

mpleti funt
ndi puer
nomen ejus

uit omnia
n Domini,
am in ci-
t.
at, & cor-
plenus fa-

s effet an-
ndentibus
fecundum

ribus dies,
nfit Jefus
& non
ter ejus.
em illum
unt dici
cum in

tes eum,
rufalem,

French (middle column):

En ce tems-là, on publia un Edit de la part de César-Auguste, pour faire un dénombrement des habitans de toute la terre.

2. Ce dénombrement se fit, avant que Quirinus fût Gouverneur de Syrie.

3. Ainsi tous alloient pour être enregistrés, chacun dans sa ville.

4. Joseph aussi monta de Galilée en Judée, de la ville de Nazareth, à la ville de David, nommé Beth-léhem, parce qu'il étoit de la maison et de la famille de David;

5. Pour être enregistrés avec Marie son épouse, qui étoit enceinte.

6. Et pendant qu'ils étoient là, le tems auquel elle devoit accoucher arriva.

7. Et elle mit au monde son Fils premier-né, et elle l'emmaillotta, et le coucha dans une crèche, parce qu'il n'y avoit point de place pour eux dans l'hôtellerie.

21. Quand les huit jours furent accomplis pour circoncire l'enfant, il fut appelé JESUS,

39. Et après qu'ils eurent accompli tout ce qui est ordonné par la Loi du Seigneur, ils retournèrent en Galilée, à Nazareth, qui étoit leur ville.

40. Cependant l'enfant croissoit et se fortifioit en esprit, étant rempli de sagesse

42. Et quand il eut atteint l'âge de douze ans, ils montèrent à Jérusalem, selon la coutume de la fête.

43. Lorsque les jours *de la fête* furent achevés, comme ils s'en retournoient, l'enfant Jésus demeura dans Jérusalem; et Joseph et sa mère ne s'en aperçurent point.

44. Mais pensant qu'il étoit en la compagnie de ceux qui faisoient le voyage avec eux, ils marchèrent une journée, et ils le cherchèrent parmi *leurs* parens et ceux de leur connoissance;

45. Et ne le trouvant point, ils retournèrent à Jérusalem, pour l'y chercher.

English (right column):

AND it came to pass in those days, that there went out a decree from Cesar Augustus, that all the world should be taxed.

2 (*And* this taxing was first made when Cyrenius was governor of Syria.)

3 And all went to be taxed, every one into his own city.

4 And Joseph also went up from Galilee, out of the city of Nazareth, into Judea, unto the city of David, which is called Beth-lehem (because he was of the house and lineage of David,)

5 To be taxed with Mary his espoused wife, being great with child.

6 And so it was, that, while they were there, the days were accomplished that she should be delivered

7 And she brought forth her firstborn son, and wrapped him in swaddling-clothes, and laid him in a manger; because there was no room for them in the inn.

21 And when eight days were accomplished for the circumcising of the child, his name was called JESUS,

39 And when they had performed all things according to the law of the Lord, they returned into Galilee, to their own city Nazareth,

40 And the child grew, and waxed strong in spirit, filled with wisdom;

42 And when he was twelve years old, they went up to Jerusalem, after the custom of the feast.

43 And when they had fulfilled the days, as they returned, the child Jesus tarried behind in Jerusalem; and Joseph and his mother knew not *of it.*

44 But they supposing him to have been in the company, went a day's journey; and they sought him among *their* kinsfolk and acquaintance.

45 And when they found him not, they turned back again to Jerusalem, seeking him.

FIGURE 12. *Page 1, Thomas Jefferson's "The Life and Morals of Jesus" (Smithsonian Institution)*

in the West, and advancing towards the South; and I confidently expect that the present generation will see Unitarianism become the general religion of the United States."[118] Jefferson proved to be a poor prophet in this case, but his exaggerated estimate of Unitarianism's future prospects in America nevertheless played a significant part in the history of his biblical researches insofar as it convinced him that his demythologized view of Christianity was rapidly gaining ground and thereby led him to persist in his quest for Jesus' genuine acts and teachings.

Although several factors had conspired since 1813 to reawaken and sustain Jefferson's interest in making a new collection of extracts from the Gospels, it was actually a chance remark by William Short that eventually prompted him to begin work on "The Life and Morals of Jesus." Writing in October 1819, Short, who had served as Jefferson's private secretary in France over three decades earlier and been regarded by him almost like a son, facetiously observed that the state of his own health was such that he had "so far adopted the principles of Epicurus ... as to consult my ease towards the attainment of happiness in this poor world, poor even in making the best of it."[119] Aghast at this travesty of the teachings of one of his favorite philosophers, Jefferson chided Short for misunderstanding Epicureanism and took advantage of the occasion to make an extended comparison between various ancient moralists and Jesus, clearly awarding the latter the palm as the greatest moral teacher of all. He then revealed that he had been thinking of putting together a work consisting of a translation of the writings of the Stoic philosopher "Epictetus (for he has never been tolerably translated into English) ... the genuine doctrines of Epicurus from the Syntagma of Gassendi, and an Abstract from the Evangelists of whatever has the stamp of the eloquence and fine imagination of Jesus."[120] This project, which he had reluctantly concluded to be impracticable, owing to his advancing years, would have gathered under one cover all that he most admired in the moral systems of antiquity and Christianity. But Short, who mistakenly assumed that Jefferson had been planning to publish a book, thereupon urged him in December to resume work on his projected "abstract from the Evangelists," arguing that it was high time someone separated the wheat from the chaff in the Gospels.[121] Short's plea was successful, for after reading it, Jefferson discarded the idea of a comparative collection of ancient and

Christian morality and finally turned instead to the task of extracting from the Gospels for his own use those passages that seemed to him to contain the *ipsima acta et verba* of Jesus. Jefferson never explained why he decided to begin this work when he did, but he had been dissatisfied with "The Philosophy of Jesus" since at least 1816 and probably felt that he did not have much time left before his death to make another biblical compilation.

Relatively little is known about the actual composition of "The Life and Morals of Jesus." As in the case of "The Philosophy of Jesus," Jefferson first prepared a table of contents and then clipped and pasted the Gospel verses onto blank leaves of paper, once again occasionally adding new verses as he proceeded.[122] Starting from left to right, he inserted the Greek, Latin, French, and English verses in separate columns, presumably putting in the English column before the others on each page. Unlike "The Philosophy of Jesus," however, which concentrates primarily on the moral precepts of Jesus and is arranged in topical order, the second compilation is devoted to Jesus' actions as well as his teachings. Jefferson arranged them in chronological order, closely but not slavishly following the sequence of events given in Archbishop William Newcome's *A Harmony in Greek of the Gospels,* which was first published in Dublin in 1778.[123] In selecting passages for inclusion in his work, Jefferson treated the Gospels as ordinary secular histories and accordingly divided their contents into three separate categories. The first consisted of verses made up of "a ground work of vulgar ignorance, of things, impossible, of superstitions, fanaticisms, and fabrications," which he rejected as the falsifications of the Evangelists and therefore excluded from his work.[124] The second consisted of passages containing "sublime ideas of the supreme being, aphorisms and precepts of the purest morality and benevolence, sanctioned by a life of humility, innocence, and simplicity of manners, neglect of riches, absence of worldly ambition and honors, with an eloquence and persuasiveness which have not been surpassed"—passages that in his opinion could not have been invented by those "grovelling authors," Matthew, Mark, Luke, and John, and therefore must be included in his compilation.[125] The third category consisted of verses "not free from objection, which we may with probability ascribe to Jesus himself"—apparently those in which Jesus intimated he was acting under divine inspiration. Jefferson nevertheless included these on the ground that they accurately reflected the beliefs of a man who could not be expected to have been completely liberated from the superstitions of his people.[126]

It is impossible to be certain when Jefferson finished his second biblical compilation. He wrote two letters to Short in 1820—the first on 13 April and the second on 4 August—in which, without ever mentioning "The Life and Morals of Jesus," he discussed the subject of Jesus in such a way as to justify the inference that the work was complete before the second letter was written. This inference is nevertheless purely speculative. In any event, he had the finished work bound by Frederick A. Mayo of Richmond, though once again it is impossible to determine when.[127]

If the completion date of "The Life and Morals of Jesus" remains a matter of conjecture, there can be no doubt that Jefferson compiled it strictly for his own moral and religious instruction. He never mentioned this collection of Gospel verses in his surviving correspondence, nor did he even reveal its existence to the members of his family. Only after his death did they become aware of it.[128] Until then, it was undoubtedly one of the works on morality that he read each evening, for, with the exception of a single important point of doctrine,[129] it was the one in which he finally established to his ultimate satisfaction the authentic deeds and principles of the man he esteemed as the master moral preceptor of the ages.

⟶⊸◉ IV ◉⊷⟵

"The Philosophy of Jesus" and "The Life and Morals of Jesus" symbolize the point in Jefferson's religious development at which he professed to be a Christian. Consequently, the question naturally arises as to what he meant by this term. Jefferson has been alternately praised and damned by contemporaries and later scholars as a Unitarian, a Deist, a rationalist, and an infidel.[130] Accepting that Jefferson was not a systematic religious thinker, an analysis of the elements of his Christian faith reveals that there was both more to it than those who emphasize his rationalism have conceded and less than those who stress his religiousness have admitted. In fact, it seems best to describe Jefferson as a demythologized Christian—as one, that is to say, who rejected all myth, all mystery, all miracles, and almost all supernaturalism in religion and sought instead to return to what he perceived to be the primitive purity and simplicity of Christianity.

The cornerstone of Jefferson's religion was an unswerving commitment to monotheism. He firmly believed in the existence of one God, who was the creator and sustainer of the universe and the ultimate ground of being. He was convinced that this God revealed himself through the natural wonders of his rationally structured universe rather than through any special revelation imparted to man and written down in sacred scriptures. "The movements of the heavenly bodies," he once told John Adams, appealing to the traditional argument from design, "so exactly held in their course by the balance of centrifugal and centripetal forces, the structure of the earth itself, with it's distribution of lands, waters, and atmosphere, animal and vegetable bodies, examined in all their minutest particles, insects mere atoms of life, yet as perfectly organised as man or mammoth, the mineral substances, their generation and uses, it is impossible, I say, for the human mind not to believe that there is, in all this, design, cause, and effect, up to an ultimate cause, a fabricator of all things from matter and motion, their preserver and regulator while permitted to exist in their present forms, and their regenerator into new and other forms."[131] As to the nature of this Supreme Being, Jefferson was of two minds. On the one hand, he sometimes thought that human reason (which he regarded as the only trustworthy source of religious truth) could know nothing about the divine nature; on the other hand, he lavishly praised Jesus for making the one true God worthy of human worship inasmuch as he took "for his type of the best qualities of the human head and heart, wisdom, justice, goodness, and adding to them power, ascribed all of these, but in infinite perfection, to the supreme being."[132] There was one thing about the godhead of which Jefferson was certain, however: the one true God that man was obliged to worship and adore was not the triune deity of orthodox Christianity. Jefferson had nothing but scorn for the traditional doctrine of three persons in one God. He rejected it as a contradiction in terms, regretted it as a relapse into polytheism, and scoffed at it as the "hocus-pocus phantasm of a god like another Cerberus with one body and three heads."[133] Of all the alleged corruptions of Christianity, this was the one he denounced with the greatest feeling and frequency.

Next in importance to the unity of God were the moral teachings of Jesus. Jefferson was convinced that Jesus had not left behind a complete system of morality. This was so, he believed, because Jesus died before reaching full intellectual maturity, because he never set down his doctrines in writing, and because his disciples first wrote them down many years after his death, "when much was forgotten, much misunderstood, and presented in very paradoxical shapes."[134] Yet he was equally convinced that the fragmentary teachings of Jesus that had survived constituted the "outlines of a system of the most sublime morality which has ever fallen from the lips of man."[135] He admired the ancient Epicureans and Stoics for showing man how to control himself, but he esteemed Jesus for teaching men to love all humanity, not just family, friends, and fellow countrymen. "Epictetus and Epicurus give us laws for governing ourselves," he noted, "Jesus a supplement of the duties and charities we owe to others."[136] It was the universal law of love, both among men and between nations, that constituted the peculiar excellence of Christianity in Jefferson's eyes and made it superior to any other moral system, ancient or modern. Although he sometimes insinuated that a number of Jesus' precepts and injunctions were valid only insofar as they were expressions of a universal moral law that predated Christianity and was common to all religions, he believed that Jesus' emphasis on man's obligations to be just and charitable to all human beings was his distinctive contribution to the moral development of mankind.[137]

Belief in the one true God and adherence to the morality of Jesus would lead, Jefferson hoped, to some sort of reward in a life after death. He praised Jesus for preaching the doctrine of a life in the hereafter to encourage virtue in the here and now and presumably accepted the teaching himself for this very reason. As he grew older, however, he looked forward to a life after death for another reason, and that was his wish to be reunited with his beloved wife and children.[138] He was occasionally troubled by doubts as to whether in fact there was a life to come, but, on the whole, hope triumphed over despair. "Adore God. Reverence and cherish your parents. Love your neighbor as yourself. Be just. Be true. Murmur not at the ways of Providence," he wrote the year before his death in a valedictory letter to the son of a friend. "So shall the life into which you have entered be the Portal to one of eternal and ineffable bliss."[139] Since Jefferson rejected the orthodox doctrine of hell but approved Jesus' teaching that God would mete out punishments as well as rewards after death, he presumably believed with the Universalists that in time all persons would be reconciled with the deity.[140]

Jefferson revered the founder of Christianity as the greatest moral teacher in history. He did not believe that Jesus was the son of God, nor did he think Jesus ever claimed to be that. He admitted that Jesus believed he was divinely inspired, but he excused this unfortunate lapse from grace as the inevitable result of Jesus' having been brought up among a superstitious people who regarded the "fumes of the most disordered imaginations ... as special communications of the deity."[141] Instead, he admired Jesus as the preeminent reformer of the Jewish religion whose extraordinary moral sense had enabled him to enunciate universally valid truths. In Jefferson's considered judgment, Jesus was "the Herald of truths reformatory of mankind in general, but more immediately of that of his own countrymen, impressing them with more sublime and more worthy ideas of the Supreme being, teaching them the doctrine of a future state of rewards and punishments, and inculcating the love of mankind, instead of the anti-social spirit with which the Jews viewed all other nations."[142] But since in the end Jesus was, for Jefferson, merely a man, he felt under no obligation to accept all of his teachings, though he rarely specified which ones he rejected.[143]

Belief in the unity of God, acceptance of the moral precepts of Jesus, hope for a life after death, and reverence for Jesus as a great moral reformer—such were the constituent elements of Jefferson's Christian faith and, as he thought, the faith of primitive Christianity as well. Otherwise, he rejected the Bible as a source of divine revelation and regarded it as a mere human history. He dismissed the possibility of miracles as contrary to the laws of nature. He did not believe that Jesus had founded a particular church to safeguard and transmit his doctrines. He spurned the theological, metaphysical, and ecclesiological doctrines of traditional Christianity on the grounds that for the most part they dealt with matters beyond human understanding and were all corruptions of Jesus' original message. He cited the "immaculate conception of Jesus, his deification, the creation of the world by him, his miraculous powers, his resurrection and visible ascension, his corporeal presence in the Eucharist, the Trinity, original sin, atonement, regeneration, election, orders of hierarchy, &c." as but the most flagrant examples of those "artificial systems, invented by Ultra-Christian sects, unauthorised by any single word ever uttered by [Jesus]." Nor was there any doubt in his mind as to the origin of these so-called corruptions of Christianity. He was firmly convinced that they had been deliberately fabricated by the clergy to render lay people dependent upon them and thereby increase their wealth and power. It was obvious, he stated in a letter that he decided not to send, "that but a short time elapsed after the death of the great reformer of the Jewish religion before his principles were departed from by those who professed to be his special servants, and perverted into an engine for enslaving mankind, and aggrandizing their oppressors in church and state: that the purest system of morals ever before preached to man has been adulterated and sophisticated by artificial constructions, into a mere contrivance to filch wealth and power to themselves, that rational men not being able to swallow their impious heresies, in order to force them down their throats, they raise the hue and cry of infidelity, while themselves are the greatest obstacles to the advancement of the real doctrines of Jesus, and do in fact constitute the real anti-Christ."[145] But much as he criticized orthodox Christianity in private, he never did so in public (except for a few general remarks in *Notes on Virginia*),[146] not only out of a sense of political prudence, but also because his deep commitment to religious freedom led him to respect the right of others to hold religious opinions different from his. For, ultimately, what most concerned him was how men acted in society, not what they believed in religion. If the acceptance of orthodox Christian doctrines produced virtuous lives, he welcomed the result without approving the cause. "I write with freedom," he informed a Kentucky Unitarian, "because, while I claim a right to believe in one god, if so my reason tells me, I yield as freely to others that of believing in three. Both religions I find make honest men, and that is the only point society has any authority to look to."[147] *Ecrasez l'infâme* was as foreign to his nature as *Credo quia impossibile*.

Jefferson's demythologized version of Christianity, like so many other aspects of his life and thought, resists easy historical categories. It was anti-

Trinitarian in its concept of God, Christian in its acceptance of the morality of Jesus, skeptical in its rejection of biblical revelation and church dogma, deistic in its conviction that the clergy had deliberately corrupted the pure doctrines of Jesus to serve their selfish purposes, rationalistic in its assumption that human reason was the only valid source of religious truth, and humanistic in its equation of religion with morality. In the end Jefferson probably best described his peculiarly eclectic faith when he observed of himself: "I am of a sect by myself, as far as I know."[148] This demythologized creed is perfectly reflected in Jefferson's two compilations of extracts from the Gospels, in which, by excluding all mythic and miraculous events and concentrating instead on the moral precepts of Jesus, he offers his view of Jesus as the foremost moral reformer in human history.

Herodias Bearing the Head of Saint John, *copy (after c. 1631 original by Guido Reni [1575-1642]), oil on canvas, owned by Jefferson (Thomas Jefferson Memorial Foundation, Inc.)*

NOTES

[1] TJ to Peter Carr, 10 Aug. 1787, *The Papers of Thomas Jefferson*, ed. Julian P. Boyd et al. (Princeton, 1950-), 11:14-18; hereafter cited as *Papers*.

[2] Henry S. Randall, *The Life of Thomas Jefferson*, 3 vols. (Philadelphia, 1858), 3:654-58, was the first to reveal the existence of two separate compilations. Before then, "The Philosophy of Jesus" had been a matter of public knowledge after the 1829 publication of TJ's 12 Oct. 1813 letter to John Adams in Thomas Jefferson Randolph, ed., *Memoir, Correspondence, and Miscellanies, from the Papers of Thomas Jefferson*, 4 vols. (Charlottesville, 1829), 4:222-26, where it is misdated 13 Oct. 1813.

[3] The following accounts of TJ's religion are especially significant: Dickinson Ward Adams, "Jefferson's Politics of Morality: The Purpose and Meaning of His Extracts from the Evangelists 'The Philosophy of Jesus of Nazareth' and 'The Life and Morals of Jesus of Nazareth'" (Ph.D. diss., Brown University, 1970); C. Randolph Benson, *Thomas Jefferson as Social Scientist* (Cranbury, N.J., 1971), 188-211; Daniel J. Boorstin, *The Lost World of Thomas Jefferson* (Boston, 1948), 151-66; Gilbert Chinard, "Jefferson among the Philosophers," *Ethics*, LIII (July 1943), 255-68; Bernhard Fabian, "Jefferson's *Notes on Virginia*: The Genesis of Query XVII, The different religions received into that State?" *William and Mary Quarterly*, 3d ser., XII (Jan. 1955), 124-38; Henry W. Foote, *The Religion of Thomas Jefferson* (Boston, 1947); same, ed., *The Life and Morals of Jesus of Nazareth* (Boston, 1951), 7-32; William D. Gould, "The Religious Opinions of Thomas Jefferson," *Mississippi Valley Historical Review*, XX (Sept. 1933), 191-208; Leslie J. Hall, "The Religious Opinions of Thomas Jefferson," *Sewanee Review*, XXI (Apr. 1913), 164-176; Robert M. Healey, *Jefferson on Religion in Public Education* (New Haven, 1962); William B. Huntley, "Jefferson's Public and Private Religion," *South Atlantic Quarterly*, LXXIX (Summer 1980), 286-301; George M. Knoles, "Religious Ideas of Thomas Jefferson," *MVHR*, XXX (Sep. 1943), 187-204; Adrienne Koch, *The Philosophy of Thomas Jefferson* (New York, 1943), 23-39; Fred C. Luebke, "The Origins of Thomas Jefferson's Anti-Clericalism," *Church History*, XXX (Sept. 1963), 344-56; Dumas Malone, *Jefferson the President: First Term, 1801-1805* (Boston, 1970), 190-205; M. J. Mehta, "The Religion of Thomas Jefferson," *Indo-Asian Culture*, VI (Jan. 1967), 95-103; Royden J. Mott, "Sources of Jefferson's Ecclesiastical Views," *Church History*, III (Dec. 1934), 267-84; Merrill D. Peterson, *Thomas Jefferson and the New Nation, A Biography* (New York, 1970), 46-56, 955-61; Henry S. Randall, *The Life of Thomas Jefferson*, 3 vols. (Philadelphia, 1858), 3:553-61; Herbert W. Schneider, "The Enlightenment in Thomas Jefferson," *Ethics*, LIII (July 1943), 246-54; and Constance B. Schulz, "The Radical Religious Ideas of Thomas Jefferson and John Adams, A Comparison" (Ph.D. diss., University of Cincinnati, 1973), 176-264.

[4] Dickinson W. Adams, ed., *Jefferson's Extracts from the Gospels: "The Philosophy of Jesus" and "The Life and Morals of Jesus"*, *The Papers of Thomas Jefferson*, Second Series (Princeton, 1983); hereafter cited as *Jefferson's Extracts*. The present essay forms the introduction to this

volume, which reprints in an appendix Jefferson's most important statements with respect to his religious beliefs.

5 One of Jefferson's grandsons, who was very close to him, testified as to his reticence with his family regarding his religion: "Of his peculiar religious opinions, his family know no more than the world. If asked by one of them, his opinion on any religious subject, his uniform reply was, that it was a subject each was bound to study assiduously for himself, unbiased by the opinions of others—it was a matter solely of conscience; after thorough investigation, they were responsible for the righteousness, but not the rightfulness of their opinions; that the expression of his opinion might influence theirs, and he would not give it!" Thomas Jefferson Randolph to Henry S. Randall, undated, Randall, *Life of Jefferson*, 3:672.

6 TJ to Joseph Delaplaine, 25 Dec. 1816, Jefferson Papers, Library of Congress; hereafter cited as LC.

7 TJ to J.P.P. Derieux, 25 July 1788, *Papers*, 13:418-19.

8 Edmund Randolph, *History of Virginia*, ed. Arthur H. Shaffer (Charlottesville, Va., 1970), 183.

9 TJ to J.P.P. Derieux, 25 July 1788, *Papers*, 13:418.

10 Douglas L. Wilson, ed., *Jefferson's Literary Commonplace Book*, *The Papers of Thomas Jefferson*, Second Series (Princeton, 1989). The specific works TJ extracted were Bolingbroke's posthumously published religious and philosophical essays. See *The Works of Lord Bolingbroke* (London, 1844), vols. 3 and 4. For the edition of Bolingbroke's works owned by TJ, see E. Millicent Sowerby, comp., *Catalogue of the Library of Thomas Jefferson* (Washington, D.C., 1952-59), No. 1265. Bolingbroke's religion and philosophy are analyzed in Walter M. Merrill, *From Statesman to Philosopher: A Study in Bolingbroke's Deism* (New York, 1949). See also Merrill D. Peterson, "Thomas Jefferson and the Enlightenment: Reflections on Literary Influence," *Lex et Scientia*, XI (1975), 103-7.

11 Wilson, ed., *Jefferson's Literary Commonplace Book*, 25, 55.

12 Same, 31.

13 Same, 42, 42-3.

14 Same, 33, 35, 36.

15 Same, 50.

16 Same, 34.

17 TJ to Peter Carr, 10 Aug. 1787, *Papers*, 12:14-18. See also TJ to Robert Skipwith, 3 Aug. 1771, *Papers*, 1:76-81, where in the appended list of books the Bible is entered under "History" rather than "Religion."

18 TJ to Peter Carr, 10 Aug. 1787, *Papers*, 12:14-18.

[19] TJ, Outline of Argument in Support of His Resolutions for Disestablishment in Virginia, [Oct.-Dec. 1776], *Papers*, 1:535-39; Thomas Jefferson, *Notes on the State of Virginia*, ed. William Peden (Chapel Hill, N.C., 1955), 159-60.

[20] TJ to Richard Price, 8 Jan. 1789, *Papers*, 14:420.

[21] TJ to John Adams, 11 Apr. 1823, *Jefferson's Extracts*, 410.

[22] Same.

[23] Wilson, ed., *Jefferson's Literary Commonplace Book*, 49.

[24] TJ to Thomas Law, 13 June 1814, LC. TJ also discussed the moral sense in letters to Robert Skipwith, 3 Aug. 1771, *Papers*, 1:76-81; to Martha Jefferson, 11 Dec. 1783, *Papers*, 6:380-81; to Peter Carr, 10 Aug. 1787, *Papers*, 12:14-18; and to John Adams, 14 Oct. 1816, Lester J. Cappon, ed., *The Adams-Jefferson Letters: The Complete Correspondence Between Thomas Jefferson and Abigail and John Adams*, 2 vols, (Chapel Hill, N.C., 1959), 2:490-93; hereafter cited as Cappon. See also Koch, *Philosophy of Jefferson*, 15-22, and Morton White, *The Philosophy of the American Revolution* (New York, 1978), 113-27, for more detailed analyses of TJ's concept of the moral sense, with the former stressing the influence of Kames and the latter that of Jean Jacques Burlamaqui. Sowerby, comp., *Catalogue*, No. 1254, offers evidence which seems to indicate that TJ was more heavily influenced by Kames than by Burlamaqui. Garry Wills' *Inventing America: Jefferson's Declaration of Independence* (New York, 1978), 200-6, argues that Francis Hutcheson decisively influenced TJ's concept of the moral sense. Ronald Hamowy, "Jefferson and the Scottish Enlightenment: A Critique of Garry Wills' *Inventing America: Jefferson's Declaration of Independence*," *William and Mary Quarterly*, 3d. ser., XXXVI (Oct. 1979), 503-23, refutes Wills' thesis. It is also notable that TJ referred to Kames, but not to Hutcheson, in his letter to Thomas Law on the moral sense.

[25] Wilson, ed., *Jefferson's Literary Commonplace Book*, 35. The preponderance of ancient over Christian moralists is evident in the reading lists appended to or contained in the letters of advice TJ wrote to Robert Skipwith, 3 Aug. 1771, *Papers*, 1:76-81; and to Peter Carr, 19 Aug. 1785 and 10 Aug. 1787, *Papers*, 8:405-8, 12:14-18. TJ's indebtedness to classical culture is discussed in Karl Lehmann, *Thomas Jefferson, American Humanist* (Chicago, 1947), and Louis B. Wright, "Thomas Jefferson and the Classics," American Philosophical Society, *Proceedings*, LXXXVII (Apr. 1943), 223-33. For an exposition of the way in which the tension between classicism and Christianity helped to produce the Englightenment, see Peter Gay, *The Enlightenment: An Interpretation. The Rise of Modern Paganism* (New York, 1966), 207-419.

[26] TJ, Outline of Argument in Support of His Resolutions for Disestablishment in Virginia, [Oct.-Dec. 1776], *Papers*, 1:535-39; TJ, Bill for Establishing Religious Freedom, [1779], *Papers*, 2:545-53; *Notes on Virginia*, ed. Peden, 158-61; Willibald M. Plochl, "Thomas Jefferson, Author of the Statute of Virginia for Religious Freedom," *The Jurist*, III (Jan. 1943), 3-51.

[27] *Notes on Virginia*, ed. Peden, 161.

[28] TJ to James Fishback, 27 Sept. 1809, *Jefferson's Extracts*, 343-45.

[29] William Loughton Smith, *The Pretensions of Thomas Jefferson to the Presidency Examined; and the Charges against John Adams Refuted*, Part 1 (Philadelphia, 1796), 14, 36-40.

[30] Charles O. Lerche, Jr., "Jefferson and the Election of 1800: A Case Study in the Political Smear," *William and Mary Quarterly*, 3d ser., v (Oct. 1948), 467-91. Linda Kerber, *Federalists in Dissent: Imagery and Ideology in Jeffersonian America* (Ithaca, N.Y., 1970), 53-56, and Richard Buel, Jr., *Securing the Revolution: Ideology in American Politics, 1789-1815* (Ithaca, N.Y., 1972), 231-34, also deal with Federalist criticism of TJ's religion.

[31] John M. Mason, *The Voice of Warning, to Christians, on the Ensuing Election of a President of the United States* (New York, 1800), 9-14.

[32] Same, 17.

[33] Same, 17-18; William Linn, *Serious Considerations on the Election of a President: Addressed to the Citizens of the United States* (New York, 1800), 14-16.

[34] *Notes on Virginia*, ed. Peden, 159.

[35] Linn, *Serious Considerations*, 19.

[36] "A Christian Federalist" to the Voters of Delaware, 21 Sep. 1800, printed in *History of American Presidential Elections, 1789-1968*, ed. Arthur M. Schlesinger and others (New York, 1971), 1:150.

[37] Clement C. Moore, *Observations upon Certain Passages in Mr. Jefferson's Notes on Virginia, which Appear to Have a Tendency to Subvert Religion, and Establish a False Philosophy* (New York, 1804), 29. The Rev. Mr. Moore later wrote *The Night Before Christmas*.

[38] TJ's fear that the Federalists intended to establish a monarchical form of government is a recurrent theme in his correspondence from the early 1790s onward. See, for example, TJ to George Washington, 23 May 1792, *Papers*, 23:535-41; to Lafayette, 16 June 1792, *Papers*, 24:85-86; to Philip Mazzei, 24 Apr. 1796, Paul Leicester Ford, *The Works of Thomas Jefferson*, 12 vols. (New York, 1905), 8:235-43; hereafter cited as Ford; to Charles Pinckney, 29 Oct. 1799, Ford, 9:86-88; and to John Dickinson, 23 July 1801, Ford, 9:280-82. For an analysis of the ideological presuppositions that inclined TJ and his fellow Republicans to view Federalist policies in this light, see Lance Banning, *The Jeffersonian Persuasion: Evolution of a Party Ideology* (Ithaca, N.Y., 1978).

[39] TJ, "Thoughts on Lotteries," [Feb. 1826], Saul Padover, ed., *The Complete Jefferson* (New York, 1943), 289-97.

[40] TJ to Edward Rutledge, 24 June 1797, Ford, 8:316-19. TJ also revealed the high value he placed on social harmony in republics in a letter to Elbridge Gerry: "It will be a great blessing to our country if we can once more restore harmony and social love among its citizens" (TJ to Gerry, 29 Mch. 1801, Ford, 9:240-44). Indeed, a recent study of TJ's presidency argues that "the fundamental characteristic of Jefferson's personality seems to have been an ardent desire for harmony, in both his public and his private life" (Robert M. Johnstone, Jr., *Jefferson and the Presidency: Leadership in the Young Republic* [Ithaca, N.Y., 1978], 34).

[41] TJ to Mary Jefferson Eppes, 25 Apr. 1803, Edwin Morris Betts and James Adam Bear, Jr., eds., *The Family Letters of Thomas Jefferson* (Columbia, Mo., 1966), 245; hereafter cited as *Family Letters*; TJ to John Adams, 22 Aug. 1813, Cappon, 2:367-70. Although *Corruptions of Christianity* was originally published in Birmingham in 1782, TJ owned a 1793 edition printed in London, suggesting that he probably read it at some point in the mid-1790s (Sowerby, comp., *Catalogue*, No. 1526).

In addition to *Corruptions of Christianity*, TJ listed three other works in his 22 Aug. 1813 letter to John Adams, which together, he claimed, formed "the basis of my own faith." These works were Priestley's *History of Early Opinion Concerning Jesus Christ*, 4 vols. (London, 1786); Conyers Middleton's *A Letter from Rome* (London, 1729); and Middleton's *A Letter to Dr. Waterland* (London, 1731). (Sowerby, comp., *Catalogue*, Nos. 1525, 1527.) Of the four, *Corruptions of Christianity* undoubtedly had the most crucial impact on the development of TJ's demythologized Christian faith. *Early Opinions Concerning Jesus Christ* merely elaborated Priestley's view of Jesus as a human reformer who acted under a special mandate from God, and was not acquired by TJ until after he had written the "Syllabus" in April 1803, by which time he had formed a basic attitude toward Christianity that remained essentially unchanged until the time of his death in 1826 (Sowerby, comp., *Catalogue*, No. 1527). In contrast, the two works by Middleton, an iconoclastic English scholar who was perhaps best known for his attack on the validity of miracles in the post-apostolic age, almost certainly did more to induce TJ to adopt a skeptical approach to religious problems than to inspire any positive spiritual beliefs in him. Whereas the *Letter from Rome* was a study of the pagan origins of many Roman Catholic practices, the *Letter to Waterland* was basically a critique of belief in the literal inerrancy of the Bible. Furthermore, as Peterson, *Jefferson*, 51, points out, it is virtually certain that TJ read Middleton before the American Revolution, thus confirming Priestley's pivotal importance in the emergence of TJ's demystified variant of Christianity. See also n. 43 below.

[42] Priestley summarized his primary thesis in *Corruptions of Christianity*, 2:440-66. See also Ira T. Brown, "The Religion of Joseph Priestley," *Pennsylvania History*, XXIV (Apr. 1957), 85-100, and Caroline Robbins, "Honest Heretic: Joseph Priestley in America," American Philosophical Society, *Proceedings*, CVI (Feb. 1962), 60-76.

[43] The impact of *Corruptions of Christianity* on TJ can readily be seen by comparing his view of Jesus before and after he read this work. Thus, in 1787, TJ believed that Jesus had had "pretensions to divinity," whereas in 1803 he maintained that Jesus had never claimed to be divine (TJ to Peter Carr, 10 Aug. 1787, *Papers*, 12:14-18; TJ to Benjamin Rush, 21 Apr. 1803, *Jefferson's Extracts*, 331-36).

[44] TJ to Elbridge Gerry, 29 Mch. 1801, Ford, 9:240-44.

[45] TJ, Outline of Argument in Support of His Resolutions for Disestablishment in Virginia, [Oct.-Dec. 1776], *Papers*, 1:535-39; Notes on Heresy, [Oct.-Dec. 1776], *Papers*, 1:553-55; *Notes on Virginia*, ed. Peden, 159.

[46] Julian P. Boyd, "Thomas Jefferson's 'Empire of Liberty,'" *Virginia Quarterly Review*, XXIV (Autumn 1948), 538-54; Donald J. D'Elia, "The Republican Theology of Benjamin Rush," *Pennsylvania History*, XXXIII (Apr. 1966), 187-204; D'Elia, "Jefferson, Rush, and the

Limits of Philosophical Friendship," American Philosophical Society, *Proceedings*, CXVII (Oct. 1973), 333-43.

[47] Benjamin Rush to Elhanan Winchester, 12 Nov. 1791, *Letters of Benjamin Rush*, ed. L.H. Butterfield (Princeton, 1951), 1:611.

[48] TJ to Benjamin Rush, 21 Apr. 1803, *Jefferson's Extracts*, 331.

[49] According to an autobiographical account by Rush, TJ assured him that "he believed in the divine mission of the Saviour of the World, but he did not believe that he was the Son of God in the way in which many Christians believed it," that "he believed further in the divine institution of the Sabbath, which he conceived to be a great blessing to the world, more especially to poor people and slaves," and that "he believed likewise in the resurrection and a future state of rewards and punishments." *(The Autobiography of Benjamin Rush*, ed. George W. Corner [Princeton, 1948], 152) Rush's testimony cannot be accepted at face value. To be sure, TJ's implicit rejection of Jesus' divinity and avowed belief in life after death comport with what is known about his religious beliefs, and his statement about the Sabbath sounds plausible (TJ to Rush, 21 Apr. 1803, and accompanying "Syllabus," *Jefferson's Extracts*, 331-36). Otherwise, it is highly unlikely that he literally believed Jesus was the "Saviour of the World," since he consistently described him as nothing more than a great Jewish moral reformer, and it is virtually certain he did not believe in Jesus' resurrection, since he specifically rejected it as a corruption of Christianity (TJ to William Short, 31 Oct. 1819, *Jefferson's Extracts*, 391).

[50] Benjamin Rush to TJ, 22 Aug. 1800, same, 317-19.

[51] Same, 318.

[52] TJ to Benjamin Rush, 23 Sept. 1800, same, 319-21.

[53] Benjamin Rush to TJ, 6 Oct. 1800, same, 323.

[54] TJ to Moses Robinson, 23 Mch. 1801, same, 325.

[55] For typical expressions of TJ's hope of detaching the main body of Federalists from their leaders, see his letters to James Monroe, 7 Feb. [Mch.] 1801, Ford, 9:202-5; to Horatio Gates, 8 Mch. 1801, Ford, 9:205-6; and to William Branch Giles, 23 Mch. 1801, Ford, 9:222-24. For a summary statement of his policy of noninterference in religious affairs, see his letter to the Baptist Committee of Danbury, Conn., 1 Jan. 1802, Merrill D. Peterson, ed., Thomas Jefferson, *Writings* (New York, 1984), 510. Both issues are discussed in Malone, *Jefferson the President: First Term*, 69-89, 108-9.

[56] Joseph Priestley, *Socrates and Jesus Compared* (Philadelphia, 1803), 1-3, 33-34.

[57] Same, 20.

[58] Same, 38-39.

[59] Same, 46.

60 Same, 33-47.

61 Same, 48.

62 TJ to Edward Dowse, 19 Apr. 1803, *Jefferson's Extracts*, 330.

63 TJ to Joseph Priestley, 9 Apr. 1803, and to Benjamin Rush, 21 Apr. 1803, same, 327-29, 331.

64 For TJ's apprehensions over the possible repercussions of Federalist machinations during the New Orleans crisis, see his letters to James Monroe, 10 Jan. 1803 and 13 Jan. 1803, Ford, 9:416-17, 418-21; and to Robert R. Livingston, 3 Feb. 1803, Ford, 9:441-43. Several Republican congressmen voiced similar concerns during this period *(Circular Letters of Congressmen to Their Constituents, 1789-1829*, ed. Noble E. Cunningham, Jr. [Chapel Hill, N.C., 1978], 1:311-13, 323-27, 347-51). See also Malone, *Jefferson the President: First Term*, 239-83.

65 George Jackson to the Freeholders of the North Western Congressional District of Virginia, 22 Feb. 1803, *Circular Letters*, ed. Cunningham, 1:312. Robert Williams, a Republican congressman from North Carolina, also discussed the "considerable bickering against our present chief magistrate, with regard to his religious opinions" in a 28 Feb. 1803 circular letter (same, p. 327). It is significant that these are the only Republican rebuttals to opposition criticism of TJ on religious grounds in Cunningham's comprehensive edition of congressional circular letters—a telling sign of the intensity of this kind of attack at this point in TJ's presidency. See also Malone, *Jefferson the President: First Term*, 190-200, for a discussion of TJ's often strained relationship with Paine after the latter's return to America. TJ was undoubtedly even more sensitive than usual to public criticism of his private character in 1803 because in September of the previous year James Callender had published a series of articles in the *Richmond Recorder* accusing the president of carrying on a liaison with a slave named Sally Hemings. See Constance B. Schulz, "'Of Bigotry in Politics and Religion': Jefferson's Religion, the Federalist Press, and the Syllabus," *Virginia Magazine of History and Biography*, XCI (Jan. 1983), 73-91.

66 TJ to Joseph Priestley, 9 Apr. 1803, *Jefferson's Extracts*, 327-29.

67 TJ to Benjamin Rush, 21 Apr. 1803, and enclosed "Syllabus," same, 331-36.

68 TJ to Ezra Stiles Ely, 25 June 1819, same, 386-87.

69 Chinard, "Jefferson among the Philosophers," 263-66, suggests that the views expressed in the "Syllabus" were inspired by TJ's reading of William Enfield, *The History of Philosophy . . . drawn up from Brucker's Historia Critica Philosophiæ*, 2 vols. (Dublin, 1792). This hypothesis seems unlikely inasmuch as TJ did not order a copy of Enfield's work until 1805 and did not refer to it in his correspondence thereafter until 1813 (Sowerby, comp., *Catalogue*, No. 1337).

70 TJ to Martha Jefferson Randolph, 2 Apr. 1803; TJ to Mary Jefferson Eppes, 25 Apr. 1803, *Family Letters*, 243-4, 245.

71 TJ to Henry Dearborn and others [23 Apr. 1803], *Jefferson's Extracts*, 336.

[72] TJ to Joseph Priestley, 24 Apr. 1803, same, 336-37.

[73] John Page to TJ, 12 Sep. 1803, 16 Nov. 1803, 5 Dec. 1803; TJ to Page, 25 Nov. 1803, LC.

[74] TJ to Joseph Priestley, 24 Apr. 1803, *Jefferson's Extracts*, 336-37.

[75] John Page to TJ, 16 Nov. 1803, LC.

[76] Levi Lincoln to TJ, 24 Apr. 1803; Henry Dearborn to TJ, undated but endorsed as received 4 May 1803, LC.

[77] Benjamin Rush to TJ, 5 May 1803.

[78] Joseph Priestley to TJ, 7 May 1803, *Jefferson's Extracts*, 338-40; Priestley to TJ, 12 Dec. 1803, LC.

[79] TJ to Nicholas G. Dufief, 9 Apr. 1803, 5 May 1803; Dufief to TJ, 13 Apr. 1803, 2 May 1803, LC.

[80] John Vaughan to TJ, 1 Aug. 1803; TJ to Vaughan, 14 Aug. 1803, LC. Vaughan was the intermediary through whom Priestley conveyed his *Harmonies* to TJ. TJ, who was at Monticello when he wrote to Vaughan, instructed him to forward Priestley's volumes to Washington, DC, and probably did not receive them until after his return to the capital on 25 Sep. 1803.

[81] TJ to Nicholas G. Dufief, 20 Jan. 1804, LC. TJ to Joseph Priestley, 29 Jan. 1804, (*Jefferson's Extracts*, 340-41) clearly shows that TJ originally planned to compile "The Philosophy of Jesus" in Greek as well as English.

[82] TJ to Joseph Priestley, 29 Jan. 1804, same, 340.

[83] Thomas Cooper to TJ, 6 Feb. and 16 Feb. 1803 (LC), notified TJ of Priestley's death and the completion of his study of classical and Christian morality.

[84] Dufief transmitted the New Testaments to TJ with a letter of 28 Jan. 1804, LC. TJ, Account with John Marsh, 10 Jan.- 12 Mch. 1804 (LC), gives 10 Mch. 1804 as the date he was charged for the binding of "The Philosophy of Jesus."

[85] The following letters describe the compilation of "The Philosophy of Jesus": TJ to John Adams, 12 Oct. 1813, *Jefferson's Extracts*, 351-55; to Van der Kemp, 25 Apr. 1816, same, 368-69; and to William Short, 31 Oct. 1819, same, 387-90.

[86] TJ to John Adams, 12 Oct. 1813, same, 351-55. See also the letters from TJ to Van der Kemp and Short mentioned above in n. 85.

[87] TJ to John Adams, 12 Oct. 1813, same.

[88] Most writers on the subject assume TJ compiled "The Philosophy of Jesus" for the use of the Indians (Foote, *Religion of Thomas Jefferson*, 61; Gould, "Religious Opinions of Thomas Jefferson," 203; and Malone, *Jefferson the President: First Term*, 205). TJ consistently stated that he had made this biblical compilation for his personal use (see the letters cited in

n. 85 above). For evidence that he used the term "Indians" as a code word for his Federalist and clerical adversaries during the time he prepared this manuscript, see his second inaugural address, delivered 4 Mch. 1805, wherein he ostensibly criticized the "habits" and "prejudice" of the aboriginal inhabitants of North America, but actually aimed these words at his political and ministerial opponents. He made this clear in notes he prepared regarding the draft of this address: "None of these heads needs any commentary but that of the Indians. This is a proper topic not only to promote the work of humanizing our citizens towards these people, but to conciliate to us the good opinion of Europe on the subject of the Indians. This, however, might have been done in half the compass it here occupies. But every respector of science, every friend to political reformation must have observed with indignation the hue and cry raised against philosophy and the rights of man; and it really seems as if they would be overborne and barbarism, bigotry and despotism would recover the ground they have lost by the advance of the public understanding. I have thought the occasion justified some discountenance of these anti-social doctrines, some testimony against them, but not to commit myself in direct warfare on them, I have thought it best to say what is directly applied to the Indians only, but admits by inference a more general extension" (LC, f.25710). It seems clear, therefore, that the subtitle of "The Philosophy of Jesus" was deliberately ironic and that the work itself was never intended specifically for the aboriginal population of the United States.

[89] TJ to Benjamin Rush, 8 Aug. 1804, *Jefferson's Extracts*, 341.

[90] Benjamin Rush to TJ, 29 Aug. 1804, LC.

[91] TJ to Benjamin Smith Barton, 14 Feb. 1805, LC. TJ received a copy of Priestley's *Doctrines of Heathen Philosophy* on 6 Feb. 1805 (Patrick Byrne to TJ, 2 Jan. 1805; TJ to Byrne, 14 Feb. 1805, Massachusetts Historical Society; hereafter cited as MHS). He revealed his eagerness for its publication in letters to Henry Fry of 21 May 1804 and 17 June 1804, LC.

[92] TJ to J.P. Reibelt, 31 Jan. 1805, LC.

[93] TJ to Mathew Carey, 7 Mch. 1805, MHS.

[94] J.P. Reibelt to TJ, 2 Feb. 1805, endorsed as received 3 Feb. 1805, LC; and Mathew Carey to TJ, 19 Mch. 1805, endorsed as received 25 Mch. 1805, MHS, announced the fulfillment of TJ's orders for these books.

[95] Edgar J. Goodspeed, "Thomas Jefferson and the Bible," *Harvard Theological Review*, XL (Jan. 1947), 71-76, was the first to identify all the editions of the New Testament that TJ used in "The Life and Morals of Jesus."

[96] TJ to John Adams, 12 Oct. 1813 (*Jefferson's Extracts*, 351-55), expresses satisfaction with "The Philosophy of Jesus." TJ first expressed dissatisfaction with this compilation in a 25 Apr. 1816 letter to Van der Kemp (same, 368-70).

[97] L.H. Butterfield, "The Dream of Benjamin Rush: The Reconciliation of John Adams and Thomas Jefferson," *Yale Review*, XL (Winter 1951), 297-319.

[98] See TJ to Joseph Priestley, 9 Apr. 1803, notes, *Jefferson's Extracts*, 329.

99 Schulz, "Radical Religious Ideas of Adams and Jefferson," 4-175, offers the most comprehensive survey and analysis of Adams' religion.

100 TJ to John Adams, 12 Oct. 1813, *Jefferson's Extracts*, 351-55. See also TJ to Adams, 22 Aug. 1813; and Adams to TJ, 29 May, 16 July, 18 July, 22 July, 9 Aug., 14 Sep., 22 Sep., 25 Dec. 1813 (Cappon).

101 In addition to the letters cited above in n. 100, see TJ to Adams, 24 Jan. 1814, 8 Apr. 1816, 11 Jan. 1817, 5 May 1817, 17 May 1818, 14 Mch. 1820, 8 Jan. 1825; and Adams to TJ, 3 Mch. 1814, 20 June 1815, 3 May 1816, 30 Sep. 1816, 12 Dec. 1816, 19 Apr. 1817, 26 May 1817, 20 Jan. 1820, 4 Sep. 1821, 15 Aug. 1823, 22 Jan. 1825, 23 Jan. 1825 (Cappon).

102 TJ to Van der Kemp, 25 Apr. 1816, *Jefferson's Extracts*, 368-70.

103 J. Edwin Hendricks, *Charles Thomason and the Making of a New Nation, 1729-1824* (Cranbury, N.J., 1979), p. 129-83. TJ had also acquired a copy of Thomson's translation of the Old and New Testaments (Sowerby, comp., *Catalogue*, No. 1474).

104 TJ to Charles Thomson, 9 Jan. 1815 [1816], *Jefferson's Extracts*, 364-66. See also Thomas F. Mayo, *Epicurus in England (1650-1715)* (Dallas, Tex., 1934), p. 14.

105 TJ to Van der Kemp, 25 Apr. 1816, *Jefferson's Extracts*, 368-70.

106 Margaret Bayard Smith to TJ, 21 July 1816, MHS; George Logan to TJ, 16 Oct. 1816, LC; Mathew Carey to TJ, 22 Oct. 1816, MHS; Joseph Delaplaine to TJ, 23 Nov. 1816, LC. See also TJ to George Logan, 12 Nov. [1816], notes; and TJ to Charles Thomson, 29 Jan. 1817, same, 381-82, 383-85.

107 TJ to Margaret Bayard Smith, 6 Aug. 1816, same, 376.

108 TJ to Mathew Carey, 11 Nov. 1816, LC.

109 Henry F. Jackson, *Scholar in the Wilderness, Francis Adrian Van der Kemp* (Syracuse, N.Y., 1963).

110 Van der Kemp to John Adams, 4 Oct. 1813, 28 Dec. 1813, MHS.

111 Van der Kemp to TJ, 24 Mch. 1816, *Jefferson's Extracts*, 366-68.

112 TJ to Van der Kemp, 25 Apr. 1816, same, 369.

113 TJ to Van der Kemp, 24 Nov. 1816, same, 383. See also Van der Kemp to TJ, 1 Nov. 1816, same, 377-80.

114 *Monthly Repository of Theology and General Literature*, XI (Oct. 1816), 573-74.

115 Van der Kemp to TJ, 4 June 1816, notes, *Jefferson's Extracts*, 372; Jackson, *Scholar in the Wilderness*, 246-52.

116 TJ last mentioned Van der Kemp's proposed life of Jesus in TJ to Van der Kemp, 1 May 1817, LC.

[117] TJ to Jared Sparks, 4 Nov. 1820, *Jefferson's Extracts*, 401-2.

[118] TJ to James Smith, 8 Dec. 1822, same, 409. For other evidence of TJ's interest in the progress of Unitarianism, see the following letters: TJ to Salma Hale, 26 July 1818, same, 385; to Thomas B. Parker, 15 May 1819, same, 386-87; to Jared Sparks, 4 Nov. 1820, same, 401-2; to Timothy Pickering, 27 Feb. 1821, same, 402-3; to Thomas Whittemore, 5 June 1822, same, 404-6; to Benjamin Waterhouse, 26 June 1822, 19 July 1822, Ford, 12:241-43; to John Davis, 18 Jan. 1824, *Jefferson's Extracts*, 413-14; and to George Thatcher, 26 Jan. 1824, same, 414-15.

Conrad Wright, *The Beginnings of Unitarianism in America* (Boston, 1955), 201-2, points out that the two leading forms of anti-Trinitarianism among Unitarians were Arianism, which held that Jesus was less than a god but more than a man, and Socinianism, which held that Jesus was more than a man but less than a god—a crucial difference in emphasis. TJ was neither an Arian nor a Socinian. Unlike the Arians, he did not believe that God had created Jesus before the world, and, in contrast to the Socinians, he did not believe that Jesus was a divinely inspired moral teacher who had been empowered by God to work miracles and rise from the dead. On the contrary, TJ viewed Jesus in a humanistic light as a mortal man who was an inspired moral reformer endowed with great natural gifts, and thus he rejected the Trinity for reasons different from those advanced by most Unitarians of his time.

[119] William Short to TJ, 21 Oct. 1819, MHS. See also George G. Shackelford, Jefferson's *Adoptive Son: The Life of William Short* (Lexington, 1993).

[120] TJ to William Short, 31 Oct. 1819, *Jefferson's Extracts*, 389.

[121] William Short to TJ, 1 Dec. 1819, LC.

[122] This is the inescapable conclusion to be drawn from the surviving fragmentary draft table of contents for "The Life and Morals of Jesus" (LC: TJ Papers, f. 42080).

[123] This conclusion is based on a careful comparison of "The Life and Morals of Jesus" with Archbishop Newcome's *Harmony in Greek*—a work that was part of TJ's last library (Catalogue: President Jefferson's Library, Washington, D.C., 1829, lot 507).

[124] TJ to William Short, 4 Aug. 1820, *Jefferson's Extracts*, 396.

[125] Same.

[126] Same.

[127] Mayo's label appears on the inner cover of the bound "Life and Morals of Jesus." Unfortunately, no mention of the binding of this work exists in the surviving correspondence between TJ and Mayo.

[128] Thomas Jefferson Randolph to Henry S. Randall, undated, Randall, *Life of Jefferson*, 3:672.

[129] The point in question was whether Jesus was a materialist or a spiritualist. TJ believed that Jesus was a spiritualist until Thomas Cooper convinced him otherwise in 1823 (TJ to

William Short, 13 Apr. 1820, *Jefferson's Extracts*, 391-92; and TJ to Thomas Cooper, 11 Dec. 1823). Koch, *Philosophy of Jefferson*, 36, concludes that TJ's "understanding of materialism was not profound." TJ wrote in 1819 that "I never go to bed without an hour, or half hour's previous reading of something moral, whereon to ruminate in the intervals of sleep" (TJ to Vine Utley, 21 Mch. 1819, Ford, 12:117-18).

[130] Gould, "Religious Opinions of Thomas Jefferson," 199, and Foote, *Religion of Thomas Jefferson*, 69-76, view TJ as a Unitarian; Koch, *Philosophy of Jefferson*, 37, and Schulz, "Radical Religious Ideas of Adams and Jefferson," 279, as a Deist; Knoles, "Religious Ideas of Thomas Jefferson," 188, as a rationalist; and Mason, *Voice of Warning*, 8, as an infidel.

[131] TJ to John Adams, 11 Apr. 1823, *Jefferson's Extracts*, 411.

[132] Same; TJ to William Short, 4 Aug. 1820, same, 396.

[133] TJ to James Smith, 8 Dec. 1822, same, 409. For other expressions of TJ's anti-Trinitarianism, see his letters to J.P.P. Derieux, 25 July 1788, *Papers*, 13:418-19; to John Adams, 22 Aug. 1813, *Jefferson's Extracts*, 346; to William Canby, 18 Sep. 1813, same 349-51; to Francis Adrian Van der Kemp, 30 July 1816, same, 374-75; to Timothy Pickering, 27 Feb. 1821, same, 402-4; and to John Adams, 11 Apr. 1823, same, 410-13.

[134] TJ to Joseph Priestley, 9 Apr. 1803, same, 328; "Syllabus," [21 Apr. 1803], same, 332-34.

[135] TJ to William Short, 31 Oct. 1819, same, 388.

[136] Same.

[137] "Syllabus," [21 Apr. 1803], same, 332-34; TJ to James Fishback, 27 Sep. 1809, same, 343-44; TJ to John Adams, 11 Jan. 1817, 5 May 1817, Cappon, 2:505-6, 512-14.

[138] "Syllabus," [21 Apr. 1803], *Jefferson's Extracts*, 332-34; TJ to John Adams, 13 Nov. 1818, 14 Mch. 1820, 8 Jan. 1825, Cappon, 2:529, 561-63, 605-6.

[139] TJ to Thomas Jefferson Smith, 21 Feb. 1825, Ford, 12:405-6. Smith was the son of TJ's good friends Samuel Harrison Smith and Margaret Bayard Smith; see TJ to Margaret Bayard Smith, 6 Aug. 1816, notes, *Jefferson's Extracts*, 377. Notice the element of ambiguity in a poem TJ wrote shortly before his death, which states in part: "I go to my fathers; I welcome the shore, / which crowns all my hopes, or which buries my cares" (TJ to Martha Jefferson Randolph, [2 July 1826]). See also Randall, *Life of Jefferson*, 3:545.

[140] TJ to Van der Kemp, 1 May 1817 (LC) explicitly rejects the traditional Christian concept of hell as a state of eternal punishment.

[141] TJ to William Short, 4 Aug. 1820, *Jefferson's Extracts*, 397.

[142] TJ to George Thacher, 26 Jan. 1824, same, 414.

[143] TJ explicitly rejected Jesus' "spiritualism" and his willingness to accept "repentance" alone as sufficient for the forgiveness of sins. To the first TJ opposed his own materialism and to the second, his insistence on "a counterpoise of good works to redeem [sin]" (TJ to William Short, 13 Apr. 1820, same, 392). He also rejected by implication Jesus' doctrine

that God punishes some sinners into eternity; see the letter to Van der Kemp cited above in n. 139. These are the only points on which TJ is known to have differed with what he regarded as Jesus' authentic teachings, as opposed to those of the various Christian churches.

[144] TJ to William Short, 31 Oct. 1819, n. 3, same, 391.

[145] TJ to William Baldwin, 19 Jan. 1810, same, 345.

[146] *Notes on Virginia,* ed. Peden, 159-61.

[147] TJ to James Smith, 8 Dec. 1822, *Jefferson's Extracts,* 409.

[148] TJ to Ezra Stiles Ely, 25 June 1819, same, 387.